As Iron Sharpens Iron

As Iron Sharpens Iron

Listening to the Various Voices of Scripture

EDITED BY
JULIE M. SMITH

GREG KOFFORD BOOKS
SALT LAKE CITY, 2016

Greg Kofford Books
P.O. Box 1362
Draper, UT 84020
www.gregkofford.com
facebook.com/gkbooks

Also available in ebook.

2020   19   18   17   16   5   4   3   2   1

Library of Congress Control Number: 2016941419

Contents

Introduction

Julie M. Smith

Matthew Richard Schlimm's *This Strange and Sacred Scripture: Wrestling with the Old Testament and Its Oddities* made a big impression on me. It's a solid entry in the swelling genre of books that attempt to make the Bible's weird bits more palatable to a modern reader, but one part of the book in particular grabbed me and wouldn't let go. Weeks after reading it, I was still pondering a very brief portion of the book—it was just a page or two—which consisted of a dialogue between Ezra and Ruth. This dialogue was completely fictional; Ruth and Ezra were not even alive at the same time. But this invented conversation hewed closely to what is known of them from the biblical texts, where it is recorded that Ezra insisted that all of the Israelite men divorce their foreign wives[1] and Ruth, of course, *was* a foreign wife.[2] Given that profound disagreement on such a fundamental manner, they certainly would have had plenty to talk about! In Schlimm's dialogue, Ezra and Ruth present the arguments in favor of their respective positions regarding what today we would call interfaith marriages. They both advocate for their positions with clarity and charity. There is no "winner" here—just a wrestle with the complexities of marriage outside of the covenant. And in Schlimm's dialogue, these complexities were not hidden beneath a veneer of sprawling academic prose but were rather presented in a reader-friendly fashion.

I think the main reason why I was so taken by Ruth and Ezra's dialogue is that it modeled some important principles in the interpretation of scripture—principles which often get lost in the rush to find a personal application for the text. One of these principles, perhaps the most significant, is that not all scripture texts agree with each other. This is to be expected, since no writer of scripture has been freed from the confines of his (or, perhaps, *her*) fallen state, so we should expect none to have written perfectly. Joseph Smith lamented "the little narrow prison almost as it were totel [sic] darkness of paper pen and ink and a crooked broken scat-

---

1. See Ezra 9–10.
2. See Ruth 4.

tered and imperfect language."[3] There is no reason to think that scripture writers, even when acting under inspiration, were able to burst the bounds of this prison. Rather, we have evidence that they were all too aware of their limitations and bemoaned them. The very title page of the Book of Mormon warns the audience that there may be faults therein. This warning is repeated by Nephi,[4] and Moroni recognized his "imperfections" and pleads with his audience not to condemn him for them.[5]

Each scripture writer also wrote from behind the blinders of a given cultural perspective; none perfectly transcended those limits. For example, Helaman 7:7 states that during Lehi's day, "his people [were] easy to be entreated, firm to keep the commandments of God, and slow to be led to do iniquity." One can imagine father Lehi smiling ruefully at this idealized portrayal where nostalgic yearning has overtaken historical accuracy. Similarly, Paul assumes that short hair on a man and long hair on a woman is such a natural and obvious state that it can serve as the undisputed premise of his theological argument.[6] Of course, current cultural assumptions shape interpretation today and are perhaps all the more dangerous because they go unrecognized.

But it is not just being part of a fallen world and being embedded in a distinct human culture that circumscribe scripture writers. The Mormon claim to an ongoing Restoration requires that various authors will more— or less—completely reflect the truths of the gospel. For all of these reasons, we are being unfaithful to the scriptures when we treat them as if they were perfect, and one natural result of their imperfections is that various texts will not agree with each other. The casual reader may never notice these divergences, but the closer reader surely will.

What, then, is the close reader to do with these discrepancies? Historically, the most common response has been to gloss over them as quickly as possible, often by adopting elaborate theories which explain why there is not, despite appearances, any divergence at all. This may be a necessary exercise for those with a theological commitment to scriptural inerrancy, but this group does not include Latter-day Saints. What if we considered these differing viewpoints to be—to borrow a metaphor from the tech world—not a bug but a feature? For example, even the casual read-

---

3. Joseph Smith to William W. Phelps, 27 Nov. 1832, in Joseph Smith, "Letter Book A," 1832–1835, Joseph Smith Collection, LDS Church History Library.

4. 1 Nephi 19:6.

5. Mormon 9:31.

6. 1 Corinthians 11:14–15.

er of scripture knows that Jesus was crucified. One who reads more closely notices an irreconcilable difference between Mark's and John's chronologies of the crucifixion: in Mark, Jesus and the disciples celebrate Passover and Jesus dies the next day. In John, Jesus dies at the time when the Passover lambs are being slaughtered. But Jesus cannot die at the time the Passover lambs are sacrificed *and* eat the Passover meal with his disciples. Despite two thousand years of clever attempts to reconcile these accounts, it is simply not possible to do so. And attempts to ignore, minimize, or deny the difference can cause problems for readers who are left unprepared for future attacks on their faith based on the "unreliability" of the gospels. But once it is recognized that the gospel writers had a higher priority than chronology (namely: theology), the differences between the two accounts become not a problem to be solved but an opportunity to be explored. Scholars are divided as to whether Mark's or John's account is more likely to be historically accurate, but regardless of which one better corresponds to history, each advances important thinking about the nature of Jesus's life and ministry. In Mark, the meal is an occasion for Jesus to recast the symbols of Passover so that the site of liberation is now his own body. Mark does not mention the lamb in this context, but the bread and wine are identified with Jesus's flesh. In John, Jesus himself is the lamb. Each portrait is theologically rich and evocative in its own way, and one feels rather petty quibbling about chronological precision in the face of these magisterial portraits of the meaning of Jesus's life. The recognition that the gospels present more than one view of the meaning of Jesus's death implies that the meaning is multifaceted, perhaps beyond our understanding. Much more could be said about the theological presentation of these stories, but for our purposes this is sufficient: ignoring or denying or explaining away the disagreements in these texts only creates problems in the future, but embracing and examining them can yield profound insights.

Another problem with quickly ironing out any discrepancies is that it generally requires the silencing of part of scripture. If we were to insist on reconciling Mark's and John's account, we will end up, in effect, erasing one of the texts. So, paradoxically, efforts to create a complete harmony of scripture result in the silencing of scripture. An attempt to identify "the" biblical position on interfaith marriage will probably silence either Ezra or Ruth. Listening to the various voices of scripture requires us to hear both Ezra and Ruth, to recognize that they probably would not be in complete agreement with each other, and to acknowledge that they both are within the bounds of sacred writ.

The presence of conflicting opinions within scripture raises the question: What if the diversity of canonized perspectives is intentional? What if, instead of just being the unavoidable result of flawed and fallen humanity, it is deliberate? What if God's design for scripture is that it reflect a multiplicity of voices? What if the inspiration is in the divergence? As biblical scholar Peter Enns wrote:

> Judaism seems to have a good handle on [something that] . . . many Christians do not: debating each other, and debating God, is what God wants. We can see the same sort of attitude in the rich tradition of Jewish medieval commentaries on the Bible. The sages of Judaism debate the meaning of biblical passages, often arriving at contradictory explanations— and all of it is recorded and preserved as part of the sacred tradition, without any need to resolve the problem and arrive at a final answer. Even in their debates, though, we see their affirmations: God exists; he has given us his law; it is important that we wrestle with it and make sure we honor God in how we keep his law—even if we disagree. But killing the possibility of debate is what kills the faith. The debate keeps the conversation at the center of the community. Ending the debate, getting to the right answer, is not the prime directive in the spiritual life. You can tussle with each other and with God (and win!), and it's all good. The back-and-forth with the Bible is where God is found. Enter the dialogue and you find God waiting for you, laughing with delight, ready to be a part of that back-and-forth.[7]

Schlimm's dialogue cleverly demonstrated this, and I realized that this format was an ingenious way to explore the scriptures. I wanted to read an entire book of such dialogues, but I didn't know of one. So I asked some of the smartest people I know to write one for me! Each writer chose his or her own topic. Given the creative and artistic nature of the project, a heavy editorial hand seemed inappropriate (not to mention ironic), so some of the pieces have introductions and conclusions while others do not; some are footnoted while others are not; some present obvious disagreements while others explore far more subtle divergences. Because these dialogues are a creative work, the manner in which the conversations take place has been left for the individual authors to decide. This includes how, where, and when the discussion occurs, whether biblical criticism and modern revelation affect their understanding, and to what extent, if at all, they are able to reconcile their positions. But each one explores the various voices in scripture by placing two different characters in dialogue

---

7. Peter Enns, *The Bible Tells Me So: Why Defending Scripture Has Made Us Unable to Read It* (New York: HarperCollins, 2014), 242–43.

with each other, attempting to remain faithful to how each person is represented in the scriptural text.

Each dialogue also models civil, respectful discourse. It goes without saying that in the current political climate, polite and productive conversation between those who disagree is something of a lost art. Especially in a religious community that makes strong truth claims, the ability to engage different opinions without contention is a skill and a gift—one for which Latter-day Saints may not see very many models. These dialogues provide a template for what courteous and productive disagreement looks like. I hope that these dialogues counter the current trend to hunker down with the like-minded by showing what can be gained by respectfully and openly engaging those who disagree. The title of this book is drawn from Proverbs 27:17, which explains that just as iron can sharpen iron, engaging a friend can sharpen one's own thoughts and beliefs.

This approach of exploring conflicts instead of smoothing them over is unusual in the Mormon tradition and may be discomfiting to some readers. But there are two significant reasons why we might want to focus on these contrasting opinions despite the discomfort. First, it can enliven and invigorate scripture study; there is something inherently intriguing about wrestling with the contours of a conflict. Second, members of the church can experience a faith crisis when they encounter former church policies or practices which are difficult to understand. Knowing that multivocality has always been part of the program prepares a Saint to wrestle with today's challenges.

The dialogues in this book are somewhat reminiscent of midrash (the Jewish tradition of creative writings which extend scripture texts). But there is one very significant difference: we tried not to invent anything which would "solve" the differences between texts. Our goal was to explore those differences, not explain them away. While the dialogues are obviously fictional, we attempted to base them as closely as possible on what the scriptural records suggest that the people involved would have actually believed. Of course, we are all writing from our own limited perspectives and have surely missed the mark in significant ways. But the goal was to relish the apparent divergences in the canon—to highlight what is there without substantially changing it or adding to it.

Most readers have approached the wrinkles in scripture by ignoring them or by trying to iron them out as soon as possible. The approach in this book is entirely different: What if these are not wrinkles to be removed but rather an intentional texture to be appreciated?

Abraham and Job: Suffering

Michael Austin

Perhaps no story in the Hebrew Bible is as perplexing and potentially disruptive as the *Akedah*, or the binding of Isaac, in Genesis 22:1–19. When God commands Abraham to sacrifice his son Isaac, Abraham binds his son, places him on an altar, and takes a knife in hand to perform the sacrifice—all without a word of protest towards the Almighty. The story has a happy ending, of course. An angel stays Abraham's hand, and the Lord provides a ram to be the sacrifice instead. But the narrative does not resolve all of the questions, the largest among them being, "Why would God command a man to sacrifice his son, even as a test, and then reward him for being willing to go through with it?" and "Why would Abraham meekly comply with God's order instead of protesting loudly and refusing to murder his son?"

People of the book have invested substantial time and energy into explaining what seems, on a first reading, to be an immoral demand by the Lord and an unconscionable acquiescence by a prophet. Christians, of course, read the story typologically: God required Abraham to sacrifice his son in anticipation of God's own sacrifice of Jesus Christ. In Jewish thought, the *Akedah* has become a symbol of both ultimate faith and of the sacrifices that have always been required of God's covenant people. And yet, the questions persist.

In her wonderful 2009 book *Subversive Sequels in the Bible*, the Jewish scholar Judy Klitsner makes a remarkable proposition about the *Akedah*. What if, she suggests, God was wrong to ask Abraham to sacrifice his son, even as a test, and Abraham was wrong to go along with the command? And what if later Jewish writers, knowing that the story sent the wrong message, created a "subversive sequel" to the story—a refashioning of the original narrative designed to correct its mistaken understanding of God and human responsibility? Klitsner believes that this is precisely what happened, and that the subversive sequel to the story of the *Akedah* was the Book of Job.

The writer of Job, as Klitsner points out, consciously incorporates surface elements of the Abraham story into the narrative. For example, several of Abraham's named kinsmen—such as Uz, Buz, and Cased—are repurposed in the Job story as place names. More importantly, though, both stories feature "God-fearing men who face a mortal threat by God to their offspring."[1] As they deal with these crises, the two men enact and embody very different forms of faith. Abraham's faith proceeds from perfect trust in a God with whom he has made a solemn covenant. Job's faith, on the other hand, takes the form of resignation to a greater power, with perhaps the hint of ultimate justice that Tennyson points to in *In Memorium*:

> Oh, yet we trust that somehow good
> Will be the final end of ill,
> To pangs of nature, sins of will,
> Defects of doubt, and taints of blood;
>
> That nothing walks with aimless feet;
> That not one life shall be destroy'd,
> Or cast as rubbish to the void,
> When God hath made the pile complete.

The following dialogue imagines a conversation between Job and Abraham along the lines that Klitsner draws. Job, who lost ten children to the whims of a capricious deity, confronts Abraham for passively accepting—and even being willing to participate in—Yahweh's unjust demand for the life of his son, while Abraham insists that faith must be something more than angry resignation to a greater force.

* * * * * * *

JOB: I cannot countenance, sir, what you did to your son.

ABRAHAM: But surely you know, friend, that I did nothing at all to my son. Isaac lived to a ripe old age and had many descendants.

JOB: But you bound him. You placed him on an altar. You set your own knife to his slaughter. And you did it without uttering a word of defiance.

---

1. Judy Klitsner, *Subversive Sequels in the Bible: How Biblical Stories Mine and Undermine Each Other* (Philadelphia: Jewish Publication Society, 2009), xxi.

You were willing to give up of your own accord what was ripped away from me because I was too weak to prevent it. God never asked me if I was willing to see my children dead. He never gave me a chance to refuse His command.

ABRAHAM: And what if he had? What if God had asked you to . . . .

JOB: I would not have harmed a single one of my children. Never. If He had commanded me to slay them, I would have refused. I would have suffered anything rather than allow even one of my children to come to harm. But they were all slain anyway, and I still suffered everything.

ABRAHAM: Oh come now, you made out alright. If I recall, you became wealthier than ever—and God restored your children in the bargain.

JOB: Did I hear you correctly? Are you really suggesting that children can simply be replaced, like goats?

ABRAHAM: Well, not exactly. But God made everything right with you, didn't He?

JOB: I had ten more children, if that's what you mean. But that did not "make it right." It just means that God killed half of my children instead of all of them. I will never get over, or forget, the ten babies that God took from me in a single day.

ABRAHAM: But at least you had children while you were young enough to enjoy them. My wife was childless until I was a hundred years old. And even her handmaid, Hagar, did not bear me a son until I was eighty-six. I lived almost my entire life without the blessings of children or the possibility of posterity. Isaac was the great miracle of my life.

JOB: And yet you were willing to kill this great miracle with your own hand? That is something that I could never understand. Or forgive.

ABRAHAM: That is because you do not really understand what it means to have faith in God.

JOB: How dare you say that! Did God not once call me His most faithful servant on earth? Did He not appear to me in all his fierce glory and demonstrate his awesome power? And did I not repent in sackcloth and ashes when he contradicted me? In all of these things, I demonstrated my faith in God.

ABRAHAM: You demonstrated your submission to God. That's not the same thing. You learned to bow before a superior power. But you never learned to trust His goodness. Without trust, there can be no real faith.

JOB: I saw very little of His goodness.

ABRAHAM: You saw as much as any man who ever lived. You were the greatest man in the East. You had wealth, land, and family. And even after you lost it all, God blessed you again. Do you not realize how many people have lived and died in this world without any of the comforts you enjoyed for all but a few months of your life? God simply allowed you to experience, for a brief time, some of the misery that defines most people's entire existence.

JOB: You speak eloquently of the suffering of others, but when did you ever suffer? You were rich too. And God walked before you all of your life removing the stones from your path. You never suffered as I did. And when God told you to slaughter your son, you didn't even complain. You just tied him up and popped him on an altar like a sack of lentils!

ABRAHAM: You speak of something that you do not understand. Binding Isaac was the most terrible thing that I could have imagined. I would a thousand times rather have been commanded to slaughter myself.

JOB: Then why didn't you fight back, man? Why didn't you demand that God explain himself? Why did you just go along with God's plan to shed the very blood that runs through your veins?

ABRAHAM: Because I trusted the Lord. That is what faith means. I did wrestle with Him, once—as He prepared to destroy the Cities of the Plain. I convinced Him to spare Sodom for the sake of ten righteous men. But when I searched the great city, I did not find even one. And I realized then that the destruction that seemed so terrible to me was, in the eyes of God, a mercy to future generations. That is when I finally learned to trust the Lord.

JOB: But your own son?

ABRAHAM: That's the point. I had to trust God in everything—even the hard things—or it wouldn't have been faith. And I had a covenant with God. He promised me that my descendants would outnumber the stars in the sky and the sands on the seashore. I *knew* that God would keep His covenant. And I knew that Isaac would be my heir.

JOB: Are you saying that you knew God would send an angel to stay your hand?

ABRAHAM: I did not know how God would keep His word; I knew only that He would. God made a covenant with my house, and I knew that God could not, would not, violate that covenant. That was, and is, the essence of my faith.

JOB: I once thought much the same way. I made no complaints when I lost my wealth or when I developed lesions all over my body. All I ever wanted was to understand why I was made to suffer—I wanted to know why God had set His hand against me. The men who came to comfort me talked as you do now. They assured me that God had a plan for me and that everything would work out for the best. But it did not. God required everything of me, as He did of you. But I was never allowed to understand why.

ABRAHAM: But in the end, you stood justified before God, as I did. We were both rewarded for having faith.

JOB: But we weren't standing in the same position at all. You were rewarded for doing what God told you to do. And you could draw a straight line from your obedience to the material well-being of your family. You knew that God was testing you and you even understood the nature of the test. When it was all over, you had a tidy little cause-and-effect narrative to hold on to: you kept God's commandments; he gave you a reward. Oh, and by the way, your son doesn't really have to die after all. That was just a little joke.

ABRAHAM: But surely you believe that God rewards those who obey Him and punishes those who do not? What could be more basic to any belief than that?

JOB: That's not how it worked out for me. I was rich and happy, and then I was poor and miserable, and then I was rich and happy again. But I never had the consolation of understanding why. All I ever got from God was, "Can you make the world like I can, Job? Can you catch Leviathan with a fish hook? Do you know how to keep a hippopotamus hedged in a bridal bower?" I got a smashing display of God's power, but I never saw anything that even suggested a coherent connection between what I did and what I got. And I never understood "divine justice" as anything more than the force of uncontested power.

ABRAHAM: Fascinating. But I must believe that, somehow, God had a plan for you and that, being omniscient, He knew that everything would work out in your favor.

JOB: You and my comforters. That's what they kept saying to me over and over again: "God has a plan"; "There are good reasons for your pain that you don't understand" ; "God cannot be unjust."

ABRAHAM: And they were right, weren't they? God did bless you.

JOB: Yes, but His blessings were just as random as His curses. He never told me what I did wrong to deserve my suffering, and He never told me what I did right to deserve my reward. It wasn't as easy as, "obey God and find a ram in the thicket." I obeyed God as much as you did, but my children still died. God never sent me a ram.

ABRAHAM: Still, God justified you in spite of your complaints, and He rejected your comforters who had been His greatest defenders.

JOB: True. And that's why I think that He wouldn't have minded if you had questioned His orders a little bit before binding your son. If anything, my situation shows that God would rather have an honest questioner than a mindless follower. Don't you think that he would have blessed you, as he blessed me, if you had demanded justice for your son like I did?

ABRAHAM: But we were being tested for different reasons. I was establishing a covenant with God on behalf of hundreds of future generations. Your test involved only yourself and your friends. As far as anybody has been able to figure out, you weren't even Jewish.

JOB: Well, there's that. I've always been more of a Universalist. I mean, what's more universal than suffering?

ABRAHAM: But your suffering did not occur in the context of a covenant. You were no more part of the covenant than the Persians and Egyptians who also told your story. My ordeal came as a direct result of the promises between myself and my God. It showed my descendants that God expects much from those He calls His people. And it showed them that they could always trust God, even when it looked like He was abandoning them. This is something that my children had to learn to survive, as a people, in a world that would require them to endure many things worse than the sacrifice of a single child.

JOB: Well, I showed them something too. I showed them that they could never understand God well enough to use other people's material circumstances to judge their moral worth. I showed them that God's ways are mysterious and inscrutable. And most of all, I showed them that, while they can't control what God does, they can sure kvetch about Him to anyone who will listen.

ABRAHAM: Yes, my friend, you did teach them that. Perhaps a little too well.

JOB: It's a gift.

ABRAHAM: Indeed.

* * * * * *

In the end, as we see in the dialogue, Job and Abraham are more similar than they are different. They stand together as the two great examples of a God who devises excruciating tests for those who follow Him. But while their narratives require structurally similar sacrifices, Job and Abraham respond very differently. Abraham acquiesces in everything, while Job shakes his fist to the sky and questions the justice of God.

What makes the two stories remarkable, however, is that God's responses to Job and Abraham are nearly identical. God commends Abraham for his faithfulness and rewards him with the promises of the Covenant. But God also commends Job. After thundering at Job from the whirlwind for a while, God turns to Eliphaz, Bildad, and Zophar—the Comforters who have been attacking Job and defending God for most of the book—and says, "My wrath is kindled against thee, and against thy two friends: for ye have not spoken of me the thing that is right, as my servant Job hath."[2]

The final words of God are quite remarkable, since nearly all of Job's words have been directed as challenges to God. As Klitsner points out, this signals a dramatic shift in the divine perspective. "From the *Akedah* to the Book of Job," she writes, God's responses to the tormented hero have dramatically changed. While God congratulates Abraham for his unquestioning acceptance of the divine will, He commends Job for his insistent challenging of God's actions."[3]

Both Job and Abraham were tested by God, and both passed with flying colors—even though their responses could not have been more different. Abraham obeys unquestioningly, and Job complains vigorously. That God ultimately commended both approaches shows us that the Divine Mind is perhaps more open, and more willing to change, than three millennia of believers have understood.

---

2. Job 42:7.
3. Klitsner, *Subversive Sequels in the Bible*, xxiii.

Jacob and Joseph Smith: Polygamy

Mark T. Decker

Polygamy forms an indelible feature of Mormonism's public image, so much so that the boundaries between the monogamist "mainstream" and polygamist "fundamentalist" Mormons are vigorously defended by many an official LDS press release. But behind this apparent dichotomy lie seemingly contradictory scriptural passages. Since all of the iterations of Mormonism place great value on the family, the question of what a typical family is supposed to look like is not a minor one. Yet the answer is far from clear, as the existence of LDS and FLDS Mormonism clearly illustrates. All this makes it interesting to speculate about what would happen if Jacob, the son of Lehi, who gives a general condemnation of polygamy,[1] were to ask for clarification from his latter-day translator, Joseph Smith, whose revelation on polygamy both endorsed and commanded polygamy for the righteous.[2] But perhaps a larger benefit of placing Jacob in conversation with Joseph is that it allows us to think about a fundamental question about commandments as well as the laws that order the secular world: What is the relationship between the exception and the rule? What does it mean to dedicate your life to keeping commandments when those commandments have exceptions that can radically reconfigure normative notions of proper behavior?

* * * * * * *

JACOB: Brother Joseph, I have a serious question for you.

JOSEPH: Ask, Brother Jacob, ask. I always enjoy our discussions.

---

1. See Jacob 2.
2. See Doctrine and Covenants 132.

JACOB: So do I Joseph, so do I. But right now I really want to know what you thought I meant in the second chapter of my book. I want to know what you thought when I said that even though God himself had told me that I had to speak to everyone about the men who were justifying themselves in taking additional wives and concubines, I felt that polygamy is such an unseemly subject that I worried that my sermon would trouble the women and children who were present?[3]

JOSEPH: Well, initially I just wanted to make sure I was getting the translation right.

JACOB: Of course you did, but what did you think later? After you implemented the principle?

JOSEPH: I suppose you had my sympathy. After all, the kind of polygamy that was practiced in your day was not authorized by the Lord. I wasn't surprised that God was upset because the selfish actions of the men you were actually addressing hurt the women and children who had to hear you.[4]

JACOB: The way polygamy was practiced in my day?

JOSEPH: Yes, the sinful way the principle was practiced in your day. You had prideful men assuming that God would justify them in all things because they had convinced themselves that they were on the side of the angels. The conditions you faced were very trying. I can't help wondering, however, if that chapter of your book isn't really about a more fundamental sin. Couldn't pride and greed have been the real problem?

JACOB: Pride and greed are serious problems, but I think I make it pretty clear that polygamy is a "grosser crime."[5]

JOSEPH: I remember that, but I'm talking about root causes. As I was translating your sermon, I noticed that before you address polygamy, you spend ten verses chastising the prideful for not sharing their wealth. Wouldn't men like that also take women that they were not authorized to have?

---

3. Jacob 2:7–11.
4. Jacob 2:31–35.
5. Jacob 2:22.

JACOB: Not authorized?

JOSEPH: Yes; not authorized, not given permission from the Lord. Not allowed to practice the principle.

JACOB: But you make having more than one wife sound like just another blessing that you can ask the Lord to give you. The same as asking for more crops or more animals or a long stretch of favorable weather. But I don't think that's what people were supposed to take away from my sermon. That's not what I took away from the revelation that I based the sermon on.

JOSEPH: But you are familiar with the law and the prophets, and so you know that having more than one wife was not unusu . . .

JACOB: Yes, Brother Joseph, I remember reading about Father Abraham. But I also remember that the Lord willed me to tell my people that David and Solomon's actions were an "abomination."[6]

JOSEPH: And that's why I later wrote that David is going to experience damnation in the next life.[7]

JACOB: For having many wives or for murdering Uriah?

JOSEPH: Of course the Lord had to punish David for murdering Uriah, but I don't really think discussing that specific sin will bring clarity to our conversation. What will bring clarity is realizing that David was not in trouble for polygamy in and of itself. The ancient polygamy of David, Solomon, and the Lord's other servants was not necessarily sinful unless they took wives that were not given them by the Lord.[8] Samuel makes this very clear when he tells David that he could have had more wives if he had asked, but he took Uriah's wife without authorization.[9] Because the Lord does not receive offerings that he does not appoint,[10] the Lord could never be happy with David's taking of Bathsheba.

---

6. Jacob 2:24.
7. Doctrine and Covenants 132:39.
8. Doctrine and Covenants 132:38.
9. 2 Samuel 12:7–8.
10. Doctrine and Covenants 132:9–10.

JACOB: I didn't see you consigning Solomon to that same fate, so apparently he wasn't quite as abominable?

JOSEPH: Jacob, do you really need to be sarcastic?

JACOB: Forgive me, Joseph, but, to be honest, I'm having a hard time squaring what you revealed with what I told my flock. After all, God himself told me that because the Nephites were a "righteous branch" that he wanted to raise up I should "not suffer that" they "should do like them of old." What I thought I was saying, and what I'm pretty sure that those who were there that day understood me to say, is that polygamy is expressly forbidden and that exceptions are so rare—who compares themselves to Abraham or Solomon?—that my listeners shouldn't even think about them.[11]

JOSEPH: And I'm sure that's what the people you first spoke to were supposed to understand.

JACOB: Are you suggesting that this commandment is situationally applied? Joseph, I even threatened polygamists with a curse.[12] How can widespread polygamy, something that is worthy of a curse in one situation, be just another potential blessing in another?

JOSEPH: That's a good question, Jacob. Are you ready to let me answer?

JACOB: Of course, Joseph. Forgive my harsh words, but this is really troubling me.

JOSEPH: And believe me, I understand your confusion. Both my brother Hyrum and I initially resisted polygamy, partially on the grounds of your sermon. I was paying attention when I translated it. Hyrum even used your words in a May 1843 sermon in Nauvoo to warn people not to enter polygamy. I think he eventually came around because of what happened to me, though. The Lord sent an angel with a drawn sword to tell me that unless I immediately became a polygamist and started telling the saints that they could be polygamists that I would die.[13] The angel told me that

---

11. Jacob 2:25–27.

12. See Jacob 2:33.

13. Here Joseph is repeating what contemporary historians have revealed to be a rhetorically effective anecdote that does much to obscure the Prophet's actual history

the Lord wanted to raise up seed by means of polygamy. Don't you see, Jacob? The angel was actually quoting your sermon in order to tell me that I was living in a time when plural wives were necessary. You do remember teaching that if the Lord wanted to raise up a righteous generation, he might command the practice of polygamy?[14]

JACOB: Well, there were obviously men like Abraham and Moses who were justified in taking additional wives. I knew this, my flock knew this, and so I had to say something about it. But I suppose I thought I was just anticipating an objection that was bound to come up when I told men who used the lives of righteous men like Abraham to justify their whoredoms. I suppose if I were able to go back and speak with my flock again, knowing what I know now, I would make it clear that the exception granted to Jacob and, initially, to David, was not an exception that was there for the asking.

JOSEPH: That makes sense, Jacob. But maybe the Lord moved you to say what you said with some ambiguity because he was also making sure that you didn't brick up a door that he wanted to be able to open again. The angel helped me see that your sermon could also be a justification for polygamy, and I helped the Saints in Nauvoo understand that we were to use the principle to raise up a righteous branch.

JACOB: I can see how the way I phrased the exemption might be interpreted to mean that the Lord could one day command men to take more than one wife . . .

JOSEPH: And that's what happened in my day.

JACOB: But Joseph, maybe this is hard for me to understand because in my day, and my father's day, and the day of many of my descendants, polygamy was not authorized.

JOSEPH: But Abraham is your forefather.

---

with polygamy. See, e.g., Brian C. Hales and Laura H. Hales's *Joseph Smith's Polygamy: Toward a Better Understanding* (Salt Lake City: Greg Kofford Books, 2015) for an accessible and extensive treatment of Joseph's polygamist unions.

14. Jacob 2:30.

JACOB: Yes, and he had Sarah and Hagar. I'm named after a man who had four wives. I know this, Joseph, but let me ask you a question about my day. Why is it that there is no explicit, positive portrayal of an existing polygamous relationship in the final version of the records you translated? Why are all the plural wives in the past, locked in what believers today call the Old Testament? Doesn't this suggest that monogamy was the norm for my people and their descendants? And couldn't it suggest that, since the Lord gave our records to you to translate for the present dispensation, monogamy continued to be the norm?

JOSEPH: But if you understand the scriptures, as I'm sure you do, you also have to understand that your day had its roots in polygamy.

JACOB: But such an understanding could easily include the notion that such things are in the past, that the record we were keeping was a record of a people who had essentially moved beyond the plural wives that were necessary for their forefathers.[15] In my sermon, I taught that Lehi was given the same commandment to avoid polygamy.[16] Consider how our righteous branch started. The sons of Lehi were commanded to make monogamist marriages with Ishmael's daughters. Ishmael, from all the evidence, is also a monogamist.[17] So, two monogamists, in order to raise up the righteous generation that will allow for a second witness of Christ, have their children marry monogamously. Am I missing something here?

JOSEPH: I am not arguing with you about the specifics of your day.

JACOB: I don't see how you could . . .

JOSEPH: But, Jacob, why is it hard to understand that polygamy is forbidden unless God commands it? If it's commanded, then it's authorized. And if you live in a time when it is authorized, then you can have a polygamous relationship provided you go through the right channels. We had different rules because we lived in different times.

---

15. It is possible that Jacob protests too much here; just because there is no clear textual evidence of authorized polygamy in *The Book of Mormon* does not mean that there was no authorized polygamy in Jacob's society.

16. Jacob 2:34.

17. See 1 Nephi 7:1–6.

JACOB: But aren't commandments designed to give clear directions about how to live our lives? And don't we read the scriptures to understand what the commandments are? But if commandments have exceptions that can completely reverse their meaning, won't that lead to confusion? Aren't people better off with easily understood rules than constantly worrying if their behavior or the behavior of those they care about represents sin or an action that's justified under a special exception?

JOSEPH: Are you worried that exceptions to commandments undermine the commandments' ability to give guidance to people?

JACOB: You're putting it a little more simply than I would, but yes. That kind of misreading is what prompted my sermon.

JOSEPH: I don't think you have anything to worry about because I think the Lord understands that necessity has no law, or, in other words, commandments don't always account for every situation you find yourself in. Sometimes necessity creates the need for exceptions to commandments, but what happens because of necessity does not overturn the commandments. Think about Nephi. The spirit told him to kill Laban, even though Nephi clearly understood that murder was wrong. Nephi, though, was made to understand that the occasion called for the action.[18] You don't hear many people using that scripture to argue that the sixth commandment is optional?

JACOB: I can't say that I have, Joseph.

JOSEPH: Of course you haven't, because people understand that laws have exceptions. I think that's why the Lord brought up Abraham's order to sacrifice Isaac when he revealed that polygamy was authorized.[19] It helped me understand the exceptional circumstances I was in.

JACOB: What you are saying is hard to argue against, but listening to you has also helped me clarify something else. Does your revelation mean that my sermon has been superseded? Does the Lord no longer see monogamous marriage as the rule that polygamy is the exception to?

---

18. See 1 Nephi 10–18.
19. Doctrine and Covenants 132:36.

JOSEPH: The scriptures are never superseded.

JACOB: Very true, very true. And because of this, don't you worry about the exception becoming the norm? Aren't you afraid of changing what marriage means? When you say that people must observe the fullness of the law if they receive it,[20] aren't you saying that everyone who believes that the Doctrine and Covenants are inspired scripture has received the law and must obey it? And since the Lord's followers are supposed to be a light unto the world, doesn't that mean that the fullness of the law of marriage is the pattern that the world should follow?

JOSEPH: No, Jacob, I don't believe that because I don't think the section I wrote is that different from what you said to your flock.

JACOB: I'm not sure I see what you mean.

JOSEPH: I think that we both preserved the exception while supporting the rule. Now, you barely mentioned the exception while carefully explaining the rule—your flock needed that. I focus on the exception, because it was going to be difficult for people but leaves the rule intact. When I wrote that Abraham received "all things" and that I was told to "do the works of Abraham,"[21] the invocation of a specific individual facing an exceptional set of circumstances was designed to imply that I was simply another person in special circumstances who has been granted an exception.[22]

JACOB: I don't know, Joseph. The verses you cite seem more of an explanation of the occasion for your revelation than a clear explanation of doctrine. It makes sense, if God is telling you to do this, that he would compare you to Abraham. But later passages make it sound like you are creating an exception that will overturn the rule. You go beyond specific directions to specific people when you indicate that a worthy priesthood holder can choose polygamy.[23] This is strengthened a few verses later when you tell women—not a specific woman, but women in general—that they must accept their husband's extra wives or be destroyed.[24] Doesn't this

---

20. Doctrine and Covenants 132:6.
21. Doctrine and Covenants 132:29, 32.
22. Doctrine and Covenants 132:40.
23. Doctrine and Covenants 132:61.
24. Doctrine and Covenants 132:64–66.

constrain believers to practice polygamy? Doesn't this mean that the exception has become the rule and my sermon is superseded?

JOSEPH: But more people than Joseph and Emma Smith were going to be involved in the principle. Did you expect that the Lord would provide a list of everyone who needed permission to practice the principle?

JACOB: I don't think that's a fair refutation of my point.

JOSEPH: But I think it is because I think the section implies a specific application of the permission to live the principle. After all, in addition to the specific instructions to me, Emma is told to be patient with me and accept my new wives or she would be destroyed.[25] This overall focus on the specific actions of specific people ensure the rule is preserved in my explanation of the exception.

JACOB: Are you sure that people would glean that from reading the section? You must admit that I was much clearer.

JOSEPH: You needed to be clearer because you were confronting sinners. But when you are talking to believers, isn't a word to the wise sufficient? People who read my revelations know what a normal marriage is, after all. And the section does not directly say that monogamous marriages cannot get you into the celestial kingdom.

JACOB: That's not what I'm saying.

JOSEPH: No, but let's look at the other non-specific discussions of husbands and wives in the revelation. The text says "a wife" and then "they" when referring to the couple when explaining the necessity of and blessings attendant upon the temple sealing.[26] The text also says "they," meaning a man and his wife, are promised exaltation while later threatening another man and wife with destruction in the flesh if they commit sins lesser than the shedding of innocent blood.[27] The section does not dismiss monogamy and does not make your sermon invalid.

---

25. Doctrine and Covenants 132:51–56.
26. Doctrine and Covenants 132:15, 18–19.
27. Doctrine and Covenants 132:20, 26.

JACOB: Ok, that's a fair point . . .

JOSEPH: So because monogamy is also endorsed, the revelation is temporarily suspending a commandment—because necessity has no law—but at the same time leaving the door open for that commandment's return. That's why Wilford Woodruff told the saints that he wouldn't have stopped polygamy unless the Lord had commanded it and the exception had been revoked by He who could revoke it.[28]

JACOB: I don't know, Joseph, I don't know. I will have to think more about this.

---

28. See Official Declaration 1.

John the Evangelist and John the Revelator: The Divinity of Jesus

Nicholas J. Frederick

While Latter-day Saints may consider the authors of the Gospel of John and the Book of Revelation to be one and the same John, an opinion that was held by many in the early Christian church, this is not the majority opinion of a lot of scholars today. In addition to issues such as differences in Greek and geographic provenance, scholars have noted disparities in Christology, eschatology, and soteriology, among others. There exists enough diversity between the Gospel of John and the Book of Revelation that, in the words of one prominent scholar, "there are in fact very few features that suggest that this author (Revelation) was part of the Johannine community in any meaningful sense."[1] Furthermore, while the Gospel of John and the Book of Revelation present two of the "highest" Christologies in the entire New Testament, the Gospel presents an "incarnation" Christology while the Book of Revelation presents an "exaltation" Christology of Jesus.[2] This dialogue explores the tension between two texts that both passionately argue for the divinity of Jesus yet take very divergent paths in arriving there.

---

1. David Aune, *Revelation 1–5* (Dallas: Word Books, 1997), lvi.

2. "Christology" can be defined as "The study of the Person of Christ, and in particular of the union in Him of the divine and human natures, and of His significance for Christian faith" (F. L. Cross and E. A. Livingstone, *The Oxford Dictionary of the Christian Church*, third revised edition [Oxford: Oxford University Press, 2005], 339). A "high" Christology would emphasize Jesus's divinity as "God" or "Son of God" and focus on his close relationship with the Father. A "low" Christology would evaluate Jesus in terms that would not explicitly include or suggest divinity, although it may be implicit. Furthermore, an "incarnation" Christology would present Jesus as God from the beginning, a God "made flesh." An "exaltation" Christology would present Jesus as becoming divine since or on account of his death and resurrection.

* * * * * *

It is A.D. 96. John the Revelator enters the town of Ephesus, the third largest city in the Roman Empire. The man looks thin and worn, but walks with a purpose. He travels past the elaborate terrace houses, the homes of the rich and the elite, and continues down a busy street until he comes to a small stone apartment. Looking through the small window he sees a second man, John the Evangelist, writing at his desk. He eagerly calls out John's name, and the two men, clearly acquaintances, embrace.

JOHN THE REVELATOR: John, my old friend, it has been far too long. How are you?

JOHN THE EVANGELIST: I'm well, and with the Emperor Domitian's death, I'm hopeful that the message of our Lord Jesus can now begin to spread even further into the world.

JOHN THE REVELATOR: Domitian was no friend of mine. It was he who banished me to Patmos, where I lived for nearly two years, simply for preaching the word of God and announcing my testimony of Jesus. This new Emperor, Nerva, seems to have a bit more sense. Hopefully he will live a long and happy life. But what of the Church? How have affairs changed during my absence?

JOHN THE EVANGELIST: The good news continues to be taught, although there are few of us left who actually knew Jesus. Those new to the Way largely rely upon the written accounts of our Savior's ministry. These Gospels are, for the most part, fair representations of the events surrounding Jesus's ministry, but for some reason no one has written about who our master truly was. I myself am just finishing up an account of my own reminiscences of the Savior's ministry, a record that I hope will reveal the true Jesus.

JOHN THE REVELATOR: What a remarkable coincidence. I have sought you out today because I myself had a remarkable experience during my time on Patmos. A vision of Jesus Christ, one that revealed to me the true nature of our Savior. It was as if the veil of heaven had been pulled back, and I saw things as they truly are.

JOHN THE EVANGELIST: What a miraculous occurrence. Come, sit and tell me everything that you saw.

JOHN THE REVELATOR: Well, it began like this. I found myself in the throne-room of God. God held up a scroll and asked for someone worthy to come forth and open the seals that sealed the scroll. There were seven seals total. A lamb approached the throne and took the scroll, but it was unlike any animal I had ever seen. The lamb had been sacrificed, and it was the blood of this sacrificed lamb that broke the seven seals.

JOHN THE EVANGELIST: A sacrificed lamb? A sealed book? Sounds like quite the experience. What did you make of this slain lamb?

JOHN THE REVELATOR: I believe it represented our Lord Jesus Christ, who was sacrificed by his Father to overcome sin. But I never actually saw Jesus Christ himself until the very end of the vision.

JOHN THE EVANGELIST: I remember John the Baptist saying something similar when Jesus came to him to be baptized, saying "Behold the Lamb of God." But I also remember our Lord Jesus being very open about who he was from the very beginning of his ministry, constantly revealing himself as the Son of God, even against those who lifted up stones to kill him. I wonder why he would appear to you as a Lamb when he appeared to each of his apostles after his resurrection as himself, although we did witness the marks of his crucifixion. I also find it curious that our Lord did not appear as his true self until the end of your vision, choosing instead to appear as a Lamb. I've been spending the last few months writing down some of the key events of our Lord's ministry, as I want to ensure that his words and deeds will not be forgotten. Perhaps I have been reading a bit too much Plato recently, but I have become convinced that the Greek term *logos* best encapsulates who Lord Jesus is, precisely because that term informs us that Jesus is God from the very beginning: "In the beginning was the Word, and the Word was with God, and the Word was God." Our Lord was God prior to his birth, and he remains so today. I find this vision of yours, with its veiling of our Lord's nature until the distant future, to be a little disturbing. The Jesus I remember was always eager to reveal his true self, who he was prior to his death.

JOHN THE REVELATOR: Ah, I understand your concern. Perhaps when I put this vision down in writing I will begin with a depiction of our Lord that emphasizes his divinity, so as not to give my readers the wrong idea.

JOHN THE EVANGELIST: What did you make of the scroll? The one with the seven seals?

JOHN THE REVELATOR: I'm not sure, but after the blood of the lamb broke the seals, I saw what I think were the events of history played out before me. I saw great men riding horses, I saw those who have died and will die for their faith in Jesus, and I saw the final defeat of Satan by our Lord Jesus, sometime in the far distant future, just prior to the beginning of our Lord's millennial reign and the building of the kingdom of God upon the Earth.

JOHN THE EVANGELIST: John, your vision gets stranger and stranger. Are you saying that our Lord Jesus's victory remains a future event, one that is yet to come?

JOHN THE REVELATOR: Yes. Everything I witnessed built up to a great battle at Har Megiddo. I saw the messianic banquet and the destruction of the wicked that would surely follow.

JOHN THE EVANGELIST: I admit I also find this a strange description. Our Lord frequently stated that his incarnation, his ministry, was the time that truly mattered. I remember so distinctly his words to the Jews, words that angered them: "Verily, verily, I say unto you, The hour is coming, and now is, when the dead shall hear the voice of the Son of God: and they that hear shall live." Our Lord's victory is not a future event, but a present certainty. Our Lord also truly said: "Verily, verily, I say unto you, He that heareth my word, and believeth on him that sent me, hath everlasting life, and shall not come into condemnation; but is passed from death unto life." The present, not the future, is what matters in the eternal perspective of things.

JOHN THE REVELATOR: Ah, friend John, but did not our Lord Jesus also say: "And if I go and prepare a place for you, I will come again, and receive you unto myself; that where I am, there ye may be also." Do the words not suggest a second coming?"

JOHN THE EVANGELIST: A fair point, friend. But I remain skeptical. Did you not also state that you saw Jesus's return being a permanent one, that the kingdom of heaven would be built upon the Earth?

JOHN THE REVELATOR: Yes indeed. I saw very clearly a new heaven and a new earth, as if a new creation had unfolded. I saw a new Jerusalem descend from heaven, in which were the thrones of both God and our Lord Jesus, forever to reign upon the Earth. It was a glorious sight.

JOHN THE EVANGELIST: But one that seems unnecessary. The miracle of Jesus's incarnation is that he already presented us with a merging of heaven and earth. He was the divine "Word" made flesh. This new Jerusalem of which you speak makes little sense when we already have the incarnate God dwelling with humanity on Earth. Furthermore, our Lord made it clear that he did not belong here, at least in a permanent state. He descended to Earth only to ascend back to his Father; he entered only to leave.

JOHN THE REVELATOR: Perhaps part of the issue you have with my vision is due to your perceptions of cosmology. Tell me, friend John, how do you perceive the universe? In your opinion, where is Heaven, and what is the Earth?

JOHN THE EVANGELIST: Well, did you have a chance to study up on your Greek philosophy during your time on Patmos? They've made some remarkable discoveries that have helped me better understand our Lord's origin and mission. Plato and Aristotle taught that there was an original, self-existent source of all life, responsible for organizing the matter out of which the universe was formed, a remarkable being who set the universe in motion.

JOHN THE REVELATOR: And how big do you believe this universe to be? Did not Isaiah say that God "sitteth upon the circle of the earth, and the inhabitants thereof are as grasshoppers?" Did Job not agree, saying that "Thick clouds are a covering to him, that he seeth not; and he walketh in the circuit of heaven?"

JOHN THE EVANGELIST: I perceive that the universe is much, much bigger. There are stars that wander through the heavens, celestial orbs even bigger than our own. As our Lord taught, "In my Father's house are many mansions."

JOHN THE REVELATOR: Yet in my vision I saw all those gathered in the presence of God. He sought someone worthy to take the scroll from his right hand. I saw the universe like a house with three stories, for no man "in heaven, nor in earth, neither under the earth, was able to open the book, neither to look thereon."

JOHN THE EVANGELIST: Ah, a universe with only three levels. My friend Luke spoke of something similar to this in his Acts of the Apostles. Do you not remember what happened to those who supposed they could pierce the sky, that they could build a tower high enough to reach the heavens? An impossible task.

JOHN THE REVELATOR: I don't know, friend John. Be mindful of the words of Job, who asked "Hast thou with him spread out the sky, which is strong, and as a molten looking glass?" I have stood on this "looking glass," although to me it seemed to me "a sea of glass like unto crystal," and upon it rested the throne of God.

JOHN THE EVANGELIST: You speak of seeing God, that you were in his presence. This is a very strange idea, for I believe that God remains at a point in the heavens far removed from the Earth, and it is from the Father that all life emanates. He is hidden, unknowable, invisible, so that "No man hath seen God at any time." That is why the incarnation of Jesus, the linking of the divine and the mortal, was such an important event. For a time, God's son, a part of God himself, dwelt upon the Earth. Did you know that Philip once asked our Lord Jesus to show the Father to him? Our Lord responded that "he that hath seen me hath seen the Father." He further stated that "I am in the Father, and the Father in me." If we have seen our Lord Jesus, then we have seen the Father. The Father has made himself known through Jesus, and that is enough for us.

JOHN THE REVELATOR: Then how do you explain that I have seen both the Father and our Lord Jesus? One dwells on a throne, the other was white as wool, with eyes like flames of fire. But I am not alone. Isaiah told of a similar encounter with the Lord seated upon a throne, high and lifted up, and his train filled the temple.

JOHN THE EVANGELIST: Well let me ask you this: How did you get to Heaven? How did you find yourself in God's throne-room?

JOHN THE REVELATOR: I saw a door opened in heaven, and I heard a voice loud as a trumpet calling to me, and I found myself there, in his presence.

JOHN THE EVANGELIST: Ah, but do you not remember the words of our Lord Jesus? He also spoke of doors through which we pass to find the Father. But it was not a door like you describe. Rather, he stated that "I am the door: by me if any man enter in, he shall be saved, and shall go in and out, and find pasture." It's that simple. We encounter the Father when we believe in Jesus, not through a vision.

JOHN THE REVELATOR: A fair point, friend John. But do not be so quick to dismiss my experiences. You speak as if the Father is far removed and that the ministry of our Lord Jesus has been completed, that his purpose for coming to Earth has been fulfilled and that he has removed himself far from this world. But when our Lord spoke to me during my vision, he identified himself as "Alpha and Omega, the beginning and the ending, which is, and which was, and which is to come, the Almighty." Is it not possible that our Lord's ministry, his death and resurrection, was only part of the whole? The beginning, but not the ending? Could there not be more that needs to be unveiled beyond what our Lord revealed to you and others prior to his death and ascension?

JOHN THE EVANGELIST: A good argument, my friend. But if it is really as you say, then tell me this—what was the point of our Lord's descent to Earth, if he is simply going to return again in the Future? What was the purpose of the time that Peter, James, and I spent learning from him and passing on the good news to others?

JOHN THE REVELATOR: Ah, I'm glad you asked, for this was one of the most striking elements of my vision, namely our Lord's role as Savior. I learned two important components of salvation from my vision, and when I write it down I think I will mention these first, so that when others read about what I saw they can read it through these lenses. The first is that I have come to understand that not only did Jesus love us, he washed us from our sins in his own blood. I realized this when I saw the Lamb before the throne of God, that it was a slain lamb. I then heard the song of the beast and the elders, in which they cried to the Lamb "for thou wast slain, and hast redeemed us to God by thy blood out of every kindred, and tongue, and people, and nation." In fact, my vision was filled with different images of blood. It is Jesus, the slain lamb, who brings us redemption from sin.

JOHN THE EVANGELIST: It is interesting that you should say that. I remember so distinctly a sermon by our Lord Jesus in which he invited all to eat of his flesh and drink of his blood. Suffice it to say that many left our small group of followers not understanding what our Lord spoke of. But I can appreciate the emphasis of your vision being one of redemption, although I would make a slight alteration. I believe that this redemption that comes through our Lord ought to be understood not so much by what Jesus does for us but by our reaction to him. Often he encountered men and women who asked how they might be saved, how they might become sons and daughters of God, and his response was that they believe in him and upon his name. Nicodemus once relayed to me a fascinating encounter he had with Jesus, where Jesus instructed him that he must be "born from above." Encountering Jesus, developing true faith, needs to be a transformative experience, for he is the true vine and the living water. But tell me, what is the second component of salvation you drew from your vision?

JOHN THE REVELATOR: Actually, it is one that corresponds quite nicely with what you just said, although again I would frame it in different language. I also learned that once we are redeemed through the blood of the Lamb that he makes us kings and queens, priests and priestesses, unto God, a truly transformative experience, as you put it. Again, the imagery and symbols which I saw were simply glorious. A tree of life, an iron rod, hidden manna, a throne. This imagery of a royal priesthood was so striking that I need to find a way to work it into the vision, perhaps in a few short letters at the beginning. I admit I do fear that those who will read of my vision will miss the importance of our Lord Jesus and the salvation he brings, instead focusing only on the images of wickedness and destruction.

JOHN THE EVANGELIST: Ah, friend John, that is the key, isn't it? Who has sight, and who is blind? Who can read in light, and who can read in darkness? I have devoted a large part of my account of our Lord's ministry to this very question. I hope you don't mind, but I included part of your own story, of how you had been blind from birth, until our master came and healed you. Although you were blind, you were one of the few who could truly see, while those who had their sight remained in darkness. I suppose it really isn't that surprising that you should experience such a magnificent vision. Our Lord's sheep hear his voice, and they follow him where strangers will not.

JOHN THE REVELATOR: It sounds, friend John, that while we may not see eye-to-eye on a lot, we both agree that Jesus is the son of God, and the bringer of life and light.

JOHN THE EVANGELIST: Well said, John. Well said. It has been great catching up with you. I am pleased that you have passed through your trials so successfully. I hope you will stop by again the next time you pass through this area.

JOHN THE REVELATOR: The same to you, old friend. I hope your account of our Lord's ministry can help his followers understand his true nature. Maranatha.

JOHN THE EVANGELIST: Maranatha.

Joseph and Nephi:
Rivalry and Reconciliation

Heather Hardy

Sometime after Lehi's death, rivalry drove his sons apart. Those who took his advice and chose to follow Nephi had been directed by God to abandon the land of their first inheritance and flee into the wilderness where they founded a new settlement, known later as the city of Nephi. They made "many swords" in preparation for the day when their kinfolk, the Lamanites, would come to battle against them.[1] Nephi was named king and commanded by the Lord to write a second account of his family's history, focusing on sacred events, to supplement the more comprehensive record he had already prepared. Now that the family enterprise of becoming a righteous branch to restore Israel's fortunes in a new land of promise has apparently failed, Nephi is unsure how to proceed with these smaller plates. He has stalled for a decade and tells us twice that although he will continue to write out of obedience, the "wise purpose" of this second account remains a mystery to him.[2] In the conversation which follows, Nephi turns to his forefather Joseph of Egypt, whom he has just recorded Lehi quoting at length in his final blessings, for guidance and encouragement.

* * * * * *

NEPHI: I grew up with fraternal resentments of the usual sort, but not until my father Lehi began having dreams did the intense rivalry begin. When Lehi's prophecies against Jerusalem met with strong resistance, Laman and Lemuel were embarrassed by his visions and resented the notoriety and animosity they brought; while I, believing the warning, cried to the Lord to soften their hearts.[3] In response, the Lord spoke to me by

---

1. 2 Nephi 5:14.
2. See 1 Nephi 9:5 and 19:5.
3. 1 Nephi 2:18.

name, blessing me and calling me to one day teach and rule over these unruly brothers.[4] That moment of revelation marked the beginning of my clear sense of God's favor. Your experience, Joseph, came immediately to mind, beginning with the prophetic dreams you, too, received when you were about my age. I learned from my familiarity with the unfortunate turns of your story to keep this revelation to myself. It was obvious that news of my blessing (to say nothing of my brothers' simultaneous cursing) would hardly be well received.

JOSEPH: As you well know, rivalry was my family's enduring tradition, maintained through the generations by repeatedly bestowing birthright blessings on younger siblings. For my father Jacob it began early, as he and his twin Esau struggled for preeminence within Rebekah's womb. She helped him cheat his older brother out of the birthright, as Jacob was, in turn, cheated out of his chosen wife by his interfering father-in-law. God blessed Leah, Jacob's first but unloved wife, with an auspicious week's worth of children—six sons and a daughter—in the first fourteen years of their marriage. Meanwhile, to her shame, my mother Rachel remained childless.

Despite her pleadings, Jacob (already the father of many sons) refused to intervene with God on Rachel's behalf as his fathers had done for their barren wives. And so Rachel, in her unwearying desperation, petitioned Him directly for a son of her own. Finally, God responded to her cries, and I was born. From that day, Jacob favored me as the first son of his chosen wife, and my status only increased after she died following hard labor with Benjamin. Needless to say, I was resented by Leah's sons long before the dreams began.

To my brothers, these dreams were obviously self-serving. And while the images became more grandiose—shifting from pastoral contexts to cosmic ones—the message remained the same: I was bound for greatness! My family would one day bow down to me! It's no surprise that sharing this with my brothers brought their simmering resentment to a full-boiled hatred. Even Jacob was peeved.

I can admit now that, at the time, I relished the self-importance of it all. I took both comfort and delight in imagining what it might mean to rule over those who had so often demeaned me. But mostly I was thrilled that God had chosen me from all of Jacob's sons for blessing.

---

4. 1 Nephi 2:22–26.

NEPHI: I can't deny that I too was thrilled by the prospect of being specially known to God, with promises that linked me to my greatest heroes—you and Moses. By this time our family had fled Jerusalem at the Lord's command, and Lehi instructed my three older brothers and me to return to the city to secure scriptures from our kinsman. My willing obedience to the difficult journey (and my father's acknowledgment of it[5]) was not lost on Laman and Lemuel, but my optimism, courage, and resourcefulness along the way won me some level of respect. It was an angel who started the real trouble. When things got tense, he arrived to chastise them, only to reveal what I had deliberately kept hidden: that the Lord had chosen me to be their ruler.[6]

JOSEPH: At least an angel verified your blessing to others, so that you would know with certainty that you hadn't somehow invented it yourself as an expression of your insecurities! I was only vindicated in my belief that I had been chosen by God decades later, when all that I had dreamed finally came to pass.

NEPHI: There's no doubt that the Lord's special favor increased the tension between my brothers and me. It took a while for me to realize just how deep and long-lasting their resentment would prove to be at my apparent usurping of their leadership birthright. I know that God prepares the way to accomplish His purposes—is bestowing his favor one of those ways? What do you think—does the Lord's favor cause the afflictions that follow in its wake, or does it somehow prepare its recipients for other events to come?

JOSEPH: An interesting question. While I would answer that both divine and paternal favoritism did, in fact, cause many of my subsequent afflictions, perhaps they also gave me confidence to do things that would otherwise have seemed impossible.

NEPHI: And the strength to endure the growing fraternal hatred, which—for both of us—soon escalated to physical mistreatment. On more than one occasion, my brothers bound me with cords and threatened to kill me.[7]

---

5. 1 Nephi 3:8.
6. 1 Nephi 3:29.
7. See 1 Nephi 7:16, 19; 16:37; 18:11; 2 Nephi 5:2 and 19.

JOSEPH: And mine threw me into a pit and sold me into captivity! Eventually, our siblings' enmity was such that they were willing to bring suffering upon the gray hairs of their aged fathers to satisfy their jealousy.[8]

In my case, Jacob's actions fueled my brothers' resentment, most notably in presenting me with that elaborate coat (that I wore, no doubt, with too much pride). He often told me in their hearing that he couldn't look at me without seeing and longing for his beloved Rachel. I learned soon enough that inheriting her beauty was a mixed blessing: it caused me to be favored a bit too much by Potiphar's wife—which led to imprisonment, where I found myself (incredibly) favored yet again. But so much for favor—a favored slave is still a slave.[9]

NEPHI: My initial rivalry with Laman and Lemuel was based on the ordinary issues of age and temperament; at least we shared the same mother! Although I felt Lehi's favor as a consequence of my faithfulness, I think he tried not to express it openly (maybe he, too, had learned from your family's story). It was only as Lehi neared his death that he finally praised and defended my leadership.[10] Truth be told, I was a bit hurt when he named my youngest brother Joseph, after you. By the time he was born, I thought I had taken on your redemptive role within our family, a fact that Lehi eventually did acknowledge.[11]

I think the most serious disadvantages I experienced from favoritism were of a private nature (and this is probably where I should have paid more attention to your story). I truly expected that it was my lot to prosper in every situation. Being singled out as the recipient of the Lord's blessing led me to believe that things would not only go well for me (and my posterity) but that they would go better for me than for my less-faithful brothers. What a shock it was when I received a vision that showed just the opposite.

I was anxious to see and know the things Lehi had been shown about the future of the House of Israel. I rejoiced in the vision of the coming of the Messiah and eagerly followed the course of my people. But from the things Lehi had shared, I had no reason to expect that this vision would include the fall of my posterity at the hands of Laman and Lemuel's off-

---

8. See Genesis 42:38, 44:29, 31 and 1 Nephi 18:18.

9. See Genesis 39:2–4, 21–23.

10. 2 Nephi 1:25–28 and 3:25.

11. See 2 Nephi 1:24; compare 1 Nephi 5:15.

spring! I was struck with horror and grief beyond compare to witness the destruction of my children! My seed was cut off—I was cut off—from the promises of the patriarchs before I had even taken a wife. What then was the point of my blessing and the Lord's favor? How was this just? How was it to be endured? I was undone. I had failed before I had even begun and felt the sort of pain your mother expressed in her now familiar plea, "Give me children,"—faithful children—"or I die."

JOSEPH: I've never before imagined her pain so exquisitely—I suppose because I was born, after all, and her prayer was answered. But Lehi saw the same vision that you did. He knew what was to become of his descendants, and still he had reason to rejoice. Do you remember what he said?

NEPHI: I went to seek him out for explanation—or at least consolation—but he was nowhere to be found.

JOSEPH: No, I mean before your vision. When he first told you about the Tree of Precious Fruit.

NEPHI: He said that he had reason to rejoice because of me and my brother Sam, because we, and many of our seed, would be saved.[12]

JOSEPH: And have you seen this faithful seed? In your vision I mean.

NEPHI: Some of them, yes. Especially when the Lamb of God will come among us.

JOSEPH: So prophecy can give us reason to hope as well as to despair. Would you rather not have seen?

Expectations, truly, can be dangerous things. We have to be careful not to fill in our own desires beyond what is actually promised. But you know this already. As you've said: being singled out for favor doesn't mean that we are destined to prosper in every situation.

My expectation that my brothers would offer me their willing submission was dashed when I found myself captive in a caravan on the way down to Egypt. Later, during my two years' imprisonment, I had plenty of time to reflect on what "dominion" might mean. Only in those abject circumstances did I come to realize that I was called by God not for my

---

12. 1 Nephi 8:3.

own (or even my posterity's) aggrandizement, but for the preservation and establishment of His covenant people. During that time, the remarkable promises made by the Lord to our fathers (and frequently recounted to me by Jacob) often came to my mind: "Do not fear. I am your God. I will be with you and keep you wherever you go. The land promised to Abraham will be an inheritance for you and your offspring forever. Your posterity will be as innumerable as stars and will be a blessing to all the families of the earth."[13]

NEPHI: And Jacob eventually extended amazing promises to you as well.

JOSEPH: Yes. After I saved our family from the great famine, Jacob lavished his father's blessing upon me. Not only was I given the birthright, but I also received a double portion as he claimed my sons Ephraim and Manasseh (your ancestor) as his own.

Later, when he pronounced his final blessings, mine excelled those of my brothers and even of our ancestors. I was to be as a fruitful bough with branches of posterity running "over the wall." I would continue to have strength amidst persecution, and was promised blessings of heaven and the deep, and of the breast and the womb. As my posterity, your family has received all of these in abundance.[14]

NEPHI: My soul delights in the covenants of the Lord to my fathers![15] And in the many tender mercies my family continues to receive.[16]

JOSEPH: Although many may be lost, Nephi, many others will be saved. And we have been called to be instruments of their salvation. I think both of us were chosen by God to use whatever power or influence we might attain not to dominate our brothers but to serve them, even at the cost of their resentment for doing so. To the best of our abilities, and with God's assurance of ultimate success, we are to insure physical survival for them and their posterity, to unify them in goodwill and brotherhood, and to promote their cohesion as a righteous and obedient covenant nation.

---

13. Genesis 28:13–15.

14. See Genesis 49:22–26, 2 Nephi 3:5, 1 Nephi 11–14; 18:22; and 17:1–2.

15. See 2 Nephi 11:5.

16. See 1 Nephi 1:20.

NEPHI: Lehi expressed a similar ambition when he called his sons to be "determined in one mind and in one heart, united in all things. . . [and girded in] the armor of righteousness."[17] My family was chosen to be a righteous remnant of Israel—to remain in the right way this time around. Lehi considered it my responsibility to bring this to pass, but within less than a generation of his death such unity is already impossible to imagine. I'm afraid I have failed again!

JOSEPH: It is true that Lehi exhorted his family to embrace your leadership. But he also instructed them on agency and reminded them of their individual responsibility to choose. This applies to both your brothers and your posterity. He saw the same vision you did, Nephi. Perhaps God's idea of success is larger than yours.

NEPHI: As I mentioned, immediately after prophetically witnessing the destruction of my people, I sought Lehi for guidance. I knew he had remained hopeful, and all I could feel was overwhelming despair. But who did I encounter instead? The last people I wanted to see! Laman and Lemuel were at hand asking questions, actually inviting me to be their teacher. The timing of this unlikely fulfillment of my blessing brought me pain rather than satisfaction. It seemed only to reinforce the inevitability of the fulfillment of the other prophecy—the one about their seed overpowering mine.

JOSEPH: But you did teach them and explain the meaning of the allegories of the two trees—of Zenos's prophecy and Lehi's vision of God's plan for the salvation of Israel, both collectively and individually.

NEPHI: Yes.

JOSEPH: Your father did well there, framing the fullness of God's salvation in such memorable and related images. You explained to your brethren the meaning of the Olive Tree and the Tree of Precious Fruit—and you were successful: they repented. But you missed an important teaching opportunity nonetheless.

NEPHI: What was that?

---

17. 2 Nephi 1:21, 23.

JOSEPH: An opportunity for reconciliation . . .

NEPHI: Reconciliation? With Laman and Lemuel? How could that possibly have happened?

JOSEPH: You've made a transcript. Shall we look at it together?

Note the emphasis you put on judgment, beginning with the first series of questions you asked,[18] and later emphasizing details your father chose to leave out.[19] You taught by fear, Nephi, rather than by love. Next, see your repeated use of the term "our seed." It was the right move, expanding the circle of concern beyond your own interest, though made, I sense, from the wrong motivation? But it is easy for me to judge! You, after all were still very young (at an age that I was only capable of boasting of my self-important dreams), and you were no doubt reeling from that most unexpected revelation of deep personal loss.

But how might things have been different if you had explained to Laman and Lemuel what you then knew: That both you and they—your posterity and theirs—are each blessed and cursed. Yes, you have been called as a ruler and teacher over them, in the context, I think, of the kind of leadership we've already discussed. You also have clearly been blessed with sacred voices and visions from heavenly messengers, as your fathers Lehi, Abraham, Isaac, and Jacob have been before you. And you have all been chosen for restoration as a remnant of Israel, to recapitulate its sacred history in a choice land under the watchful care of the God of your fathers. But what of Laman and Lemuel? What have they been blessed with? And what cursings apply to each of you as well?

NEPHI: Their blessing is my curse—

JOSEPH: That they are blessed at all? I'm surprised to hear that from you, Nephi! I know you have a good heart, softened by the Lord, by your own admission,[20] and capable of generosity. You've prayed for your brothers before and recognized that their limited vision is due in part to not knowing the dealings of God.[21]

---

18. 1 Nephi 15:8–11.
19. 1 Nephi 15:24, 27–36.
20. See 1 Nephi 2:16.
21. See 1 Nephi 2:1.

NEPHI: Excuse my ambiguity! You misunderstand. I meant only that my great curse—the destruction of my posterity—is only magnified in being matched precisely by their most significant blessing: the promise of persistence. As long as there is life, there is the possibility for repentance.

JOSEPH: Let me share with you the moment in my life that changed everything. It was in Egypt during the famine, at the time when I chose to reveal my identity to my brothers who had come to purchase grain. Years before, these brothers had done me a great wrong, led on by jealousy and their own hardened hearts. But I had learned much in the years since I had lived with them in Canaan, schooled not just by my service to Pharaoh but also by my many afflictions. I understood that God's favor had sustained me in order that I, in turn, could sustain others. When I recognized them on their first visit, the Lord let me know that my calling was to preserve them, the bearers of Abraham's covenant and inheritors of his blessing, regardless of any justified animosity I might still have held.

I want you to listen carefully to what I told them: It was not you who sent me here, but God. He sent me before you to preserve life . . . to preserve a posterity for you in the earth, and to save your lives by a great deliverance.[22] Although they had meant evil against me, "God meant it for good, to save many people alive."[23]

I suggested the possibility of reconciliation earlier. Your first reconciliation, Nephi, is to the will of God. To both His justice and His mercy. Don't resent the future He has blessed you to see because you do not yet fully understand it. The God of your fathers will help you and bless your efforts in bringing salvation to His covenant people. Trust His providential design—it is larger than we can imagine. He will open the gates of righteousness and clear the way before you.[24] You, too, are called to do a great work to preserve your brothers' posterity "by a great deliverance" and to "save many people alive."

NEPHI: But what can I do now? My family has split, irreconcilably I fear. Instead of a restored remnant, we have begun Israel's cycle of enmity anew. Isn't it too late?

---

22. Genesis 45:5–8.
23. Genesis 50:20.
24. See 2 Nephi 4:14, 32–33.

JOSEPH: Perhaps not. We are saved, it seems, not by doing it right the first time but by suffering through having gotten it wrong. "As long as there is life, there is the possibility for repentance," isn't that what you said? We come to God through our weakness, Nephi, and He will make us strong.[25] Pray for God to again soften your heart. Pray for the charity to frankly forgive your brothers now as you did long ago.[26] Although you are currently separated from them, you still can love them, rejoice in their promised blessings, and wait for the fulfillment of those blessings in the Lord's time.

You can also pray for your brethren. Plead with the Lord on their behalf as Rachel continued to weep for her absent children. The Lord rewarded her labor. God's blessing was initially extended to you as you were pleading on behalf of your brothers' hardened hearts.[27] Don't stop crying for them and their posterity as well as for your own. Embrace the promises to the patriarchs and leave judgment to God. Your prayers, like those of your dear foremother, can also become an effectual voice from the dust.[28]

You know the story of Rachel's tears. She died in childbirth with Benjamin, on our journey back to the promised land. Jacob buried her on the way, in Ramah, rather than travel half a day to place her body in the family tomb at Machpelah, the final resting place of Abraham and Sarah, Isaac and Rebekah, and eventually Jacob and Leah. In death, Jacob's beloved wife, the mother of the northern tribes, was separated from the rest, as her sons would likewise be separated when the Assyrians came. But Ramah, it turns out, was on the way to Israel's exile. Rachel saw it all and, practiced at weeping from pleading for her sons' birth, she wept again as she saw her posterity carried off. God heard her prayers: Your labor shall be rewarded, He said. There is hope in your future; your children shall come back from the land of their enemies, back to their own borders.[29] Rachel's weeping brought redemption for her sons. And Laman and Lemuel are her sons, too.

Rachel could only cry from the dust, but you, Nephi, can also write! Lehi was right when he taught that I saw your day. Read my prophecies again, and find yourself in them. Cry not only for God's merciful inter-

---

25. See 2 Nephi 3:21.
26. See 1 Nephi 7:15–16.
27. See 1 Nephi 2:18–19.
28. See 2 Nephi 3:19b.
29. See Jeremiah 31:15–22.

cession, but also preach repentance to those who will come after you.[30] Teach your children, and your brothers' children, and the descendants of the patriarchs, and all the families of the earth, how to come unto God of Abraham, Isaac, and Jacob and be saved.[31] Teach the points of his doctrine plainly, so they cannot err. You are to be a teacher, Nephi, not only to Laman and Lemuel but to an audience as numerous as the sand and the stars. Teach them of the two trees and of the expansive sense of salvation that Israel's God has revealed to you.

Through God's design I was able to save many from physical starvation, and you, my son, will provide the means to save them from spiritual death. Sometime, somewhere, some will listen. The Lord has promised me that your words will be preserved and many shall hearken in bringing to pass much restoration of Israel.[32] For my part, I believe Him. Write, Nephi, write! Save your brothers' posterity. Save many.

* * * * * * *

The final section of Second Nephi (chapters 25–33) is notably different from Nephi's prior writings. Here he clearly identifies an expanded audience[33] whom he addresses for the first time—and then repeatedly—as his "beloved brethren."[34] He recounts his earlier vision and the anguish that witnessing the destruction of his posterity has caused him, but this time he is able to concede the justice of God's actions.[35] In a clearly framed depiction of the "doctrine of Christ,"[36] Nephi reveals the interpretation of key elements from Lehi's Dream that were not specified earlier—including the identity of the man bidding him to follow, as well as the meaning of the strait and narrow path and how one "presses forward" along it.[37] He indicates in plainness how one is to come unto Christ—the God of Abraham, Isaac, and Jacob—and be saved.[38]

---

30. 2 Nephi 3:20.
31. 1 Nephi 6:4 and 15:14.
32. See 2 Nephi 3:24.
33. Compare 1 Nephi 19:3, 5 and 2 Nephi 33:10, 13.
34. See 2 Nephi 26:1, and fifteen times thereafter.
35. See 1 Nephi 12:19–20, 15:1–5, 2 Nephi 26:6–7, 10–11.
36. 2 Nephi 31:2, 21; compare 1 Nephi 15:14.
37. 2 Nephi 31:9–10, 18–20; compare 1 Nephi 8:20, 24, 6.
38. 2 Nephi 31:19–21; compare 1 Nephi 6:4.

Nephi also alludes to several distinctive phrases from Joseph's prophecies regarding the sacred words his posterity will write, thereby claiming their fulfillment for himself. He describes his efforts as crying in faith on behalf of his brethren, and, specifically, as crying to them from the dust.[39] Nephi further describes the words he has written as being of great worth to these brethren;[40] as being written in weakness, so that they may subsequently be made strong in the Lord;[41] and as proceeding forth from the mouth of the Lord himself.[42] There is little doubt of Joseph's influence on the final form of Nephi's small plates.

Nor is there doubt that, in the end, Nephi finally comes to an understanding of the purpose of his second record, despite the fact that he has also chosen to keep this "wise purpose" hidden. By beginning and ending the small plates with accounts of his crying to the Lord because of his people's hardened hearts, Nephi highlights his persistent concern about fraternal rivalry and the possibility for reconciliation.[43] In the conversation related above, Joseph encourages Nephi to reconcile with his brothers, despite the current hostility, by directing the small plates to Lamanites of a later day, thereby bringing Lehi's (and Joseph's) surviving descendants to a knowledge of the covenants made by the Lord to their fathers. Joseph further suggests that through his writings, Nephi, too, was sent by God to save his brothers' posterity "by a great deliverance" and to save many more besides.[44]

A close reading of subsequent small plates' authors suggests that an oral tradition to this effect accompanied the transfer of the record from one guardian to the next. Jacob all but admits that he, too, knows that the Nephites will one day be destroyed and that the record of sacred, saving truths they are keeping is ultimately for the benefit of their rivals.[45] His son Enos addresses this possibility more openly, but still as a hypothetical scenario, albeit one for whose outcome he cries unto the Lord continually.[46] Enos also discloses the reason for his indirection: the Lamanites had sworn in their wrath that "if it were possible, they would destroy our

---

39. 2 Nephi 33:3–4, 13; compare 3:19b–21.
40. 2 Nephi 33:3; compare 3:7.
41. 2 Nephi 33:10, 14; compare 3:21.
42. 2 Nephi 33:10, 14; compare 3:21.
43. 1 Nephi 2:18 and 2 Nephi 33:2–3.
44. See Genesis 45:7 and 50:20.
45. Jacob 1:1–5 and 7:27.
46. Enos 1:14–18.

records and us."[47] For Enos' son Jarom, the secret is out: "These things are written for the intent of the benefit of our brethren the Lamanites."[48]

Recognizing Nephi's Small Plates as a record kept and preserved, and perhaps even titled, "for the Lamanites" clarifies a few long-standing puzzles in the Book of Mormon. It can account for why Mormon was unfamiliar with the text until late in his editing process.[49] His own long-standing and well-justified enmity with the Lamanites coupled with the recognition that they would destroy any Nephite records they came upon could certainly have reduced the priority of the text for his limited attention.[50] It may also explain Alma's initial unfamiliarity with explicit small-plates' prophecies about the coming of the resurrected Christ to the Nephites.[51] While Alma would have had possession of Nephi's small plates for perhaps a decade at this point,[52] given his preaching efforts, he, too, may have given priority to scriptures specifically addressed to the Nephites. The timing of a seeming contradiction at Alma 16:20, when the church is informed that the Son of God "would appear unto them after his resurrection" is of particular note. It coincides with Alma's reunion with the Sons of Mosiah returning from their mission "to impart the word of God to their brethren, the Lamanites."[53] There thus may be reason to believe that they had taken the small plates with them in their endeavor.[54] Once the Sons of Mosiah return, with deep familiarity with a text they have been studying for fourteen years,[55] the good news is widely disseminated.

---

47. Enos 1:14.

48. Jarom 1:2.

49. See Words of Mormon 1:3–5.

50. See Mormon 6:6.

51. See Alma 7:8; compare 1 Nephi 12:6, 2 Nephi 26:1, 9.

52. See Omni 1:25 and Mosiah 28:20.

53. Mosiah 28:1.

54. See the similar wording in Mosiah 28:1–2, Alma 21:17, 26:24, and Alma 37:1–2, 8–12, 14—noting especially the reference to God's "wise purpose" and allusions to notable small-plates' texts, including 1 Nephi 10:19, in verse 12, and similarities, as well, to Joseph of Egypt's prophecies about his descendants' writings at 2 Nephi 3:11–12.

55. Alma 17:2.

Job and John:
The Satans

JOHN: We need to talk about the Great Dragon. You have met him I presume?

JOB: I am not sure. Have I?

JOHN: That Satan who cursed your life!

JOB: I have known many satans. It's a popular name around here. In my Hebrew tongue the name comes from the verb śāṭan.[1]

JOHN: And in English (for the sake of our audience)? Something devilish, I presume.

JOB: Let me think. The precise meaning is difficult to render in English but lies somewhere between "to accuse," "to slander," and "to be an adversary." You know Greek: the Septuagint will translate it in Psalm 38:21 with the term *endieballon*, suggesting slander.

JOHN: Definitely sounds devilish.

JOB: I suppose but it depends on who is being an adversary, why, and to whom. In Greek you have this term for "devil"—diabolos—which conveys a roughly similar meaning: "one who throws something across one's path," or "obstructor."[2] In the Hebrew tradition we often apply the term satan to human or heavenly figures who block the way of the wrongdoer, with a negative

---

1. The verb occurs only six times in the Hebrew Bible (Psalm 38:21; 71:13; 109:4, 20, 29; Zechariah 3:1) and lacks a Semitic cognate.

2. In 1 Maccabees 1:36, Antiochus IV is called *diabolon ponēron*—an "evil foe." Diabolos needed to be qualified by *ponēros* to make it clear the person in question was indeed wicked. "Devil" in English has, of course, lost this ambiguity.

sense of "adversary" or "slanderer" applied only when the satan in question is doing mischief thereby. Or at least, mischief of which God does not approve.

JOHN: So, how many of these satans have there been?

JOB: Many! On earth there was David, when he was seen as a threat by the Philistine lords;[3] Abishai, for overstepping the bounds of his authority in David's eyes;[4] a whole raft of Solomon's enemies (he had lots of enemies);[5] Hadad, the Elamite, whom the Lord incited against Solomon;[6] Rezon too, if I recall correctly.[7] Many of the Bibles people will read will simply translate śāṭān in all of these passages as "adversary."

JOHN: You said there are heavenly satans too.

JOB: Yes. Too many to name. There was the angel of the Lord who acted as "a satan" in blocking the path in front of poor Balaam's ass;[8] "the satan," (with definite article: haśśāṭān) who stood as Joshua the high priest's accuser in heaven and whom the Lord rebuked;[9] and a satan who incited David to take a census of Israel.[10] Then there was that satan who made my life so miserable, of course. So you see that we use "satan" as a title given to numerous beings, both human and not, who act as someone's "adversary," but not necessarily in opposition to God's will. On the contrary!

JOHN: Intriguing. There is more to this than I supposed. You know, your story is a horror, even worse than mine.

JOB: Really? All those weird beasts, all that blood and fire! Anyway, my story suggests something that has been going on for a very long time. So long, in fact, that we are not even sure if there was a beginning to it.

---

3. 1 Samuel 29:4.
4. 2 Samuel 19:22.
5. 1 Kings 5:4.
6. 1 Kings 11:14.
7. 1 Kings 11:23, 25.
8. Numbers 22:22.
9. Zechariah 3:1–2.
10. 1 Chronicles 21:1. This passage emends 2 Samuel 24:1 where it is Yahweh that takes a census of Israel.

JOHN: Go on. Satan cursed you in order to win a bet with God.

JOB: Careful. If you were to know your Hebrew you would see that he is described as "the satan" and not simply "Satan" or even "satan." (Those capitalized proper nouns in English can be very misleading, not something we have to worry about in our tongues!) In my story, as I was later to find out, "the satan"[11] was "roaming[12] the earth." God brings my, well, perfect righteousness to the satan's attention and grants him the power to disturb my life, to "prove" me. I guess I passed but it was dreadful at the time.

JOHN: So, the Dragon works for God?

JOB: Again, caution! I have said nothing about your Dragon!

---

11. Biblical scholars have provided various models for the creation and evolution of the literary character of "satan" in the book of Job. Neil Forsyth assumes a Persian period composition for Job (fifth to fourth centuries B.C.E.). He sees the satan's "roaming" as alluding to the spies of the Persian court who patrolled the empire, a system of control "that must have been especially irksome to subjects of the Great King and may suggest that at least the Satan part of the Book of Job was composed in Persian times." Neil Forsyth, *The Old Enemy: Satan and the Combat Myth* (Princeton: Princeton University Press, 1987), 114. In his model, the satan represents the transfer of a political situation to a theological level. A. Leo Oppenheim, "The Eyes of the Lord," *Journal of the American Oriental Society* 88, no. 1 (1968): 175. This suggestion has been made by various scholars and is followed by some of the commentaries. See James Crenshaw, "Job, Book of," in *The Anchor Bible Dictionary*, ed D. N. Freedman (New York: Doubleday, 1992), 863–64 and the somewhat idiosyncratic H. Torczyner, "How Satan Came into the World," *Expository Times* 48 (1936–1937): 563–65. Reference is often made to Persian royal spies in the Greek sources: The king has a thousand eyes and a thousand ears; and hence the fear of uttering anything against his interest since "he is sure to hear," or "since he may be there to see." Xenophon, *Cyropedia*, VIII.2.10–12. From this evidence it has been suggested that the Persian satrapies were watched over by royal "spies" who reported any rebellion or disloyalty to the king. Crucially, however, there is no Persian evidence that confirms the existence of the institution of the King's Eye or Ear. Hirsch concludes that, "the known facts of Persian history provide no support to a belief in the existence of a comprehensive network of agents relaying information to the Great King." Steven W. Hirsch, *The Friendship of the Barbarians: Xenophon and the Persian Empire* (Hanover: New England, 1985), 129. Hirsch ascribes the Greek notion of a Persian spy network to the influence of Iranian mythological tradition, particularly the "Eyes of Mithra" (120f).

12. Šûṭ, "to roam," probably a pun on śāṭān.

JOHN: Right, yes. I keep forgetting.

JOB: This particular satan was a member of the Divine Council, the celestial assembly with God at its center.[13] You know the title, "Lord of hosts"? Well, that conveys this idea of the heavenly court which makes up the Lord's retinue. Imagine it like the royal courts on earth. The Lord is the king and warrior, surrounded by his court and his army. Human courts also include the kind of officials to which the figure of the satan in my story alludes. In judicial courts, prosecutors[14] and accusers play important roles, and in the apparatus of imperial government, spies, and informers are crucial to the maintenance of the state.

JOHN: Given what I saw, it's hard for me to believe that any satan is part of God's court!

JOB: Is it really so hard? Some religious traditions have it. This idea that the Lord gave the satan a mission to this earth is not so strange.[15] He is

---

13. For discussion and references, see E. Theodore Mullen, "Divine Assembly," in *The Anchor Bible Dictionary*, ed. D. N. Freedman (New York: Doubleday, 1992), 214–17. The members of the divine court are called variously: "sons of gods/El" (Ps. 29:1; 89:7), "sons of God" (Deut. 32:8; Gen. 6:2, 4; Job 1:6, 2:1), "sons of Elyon" (Ps. 82:6), "all the gods" (Ps. 97:7), "holy ones" (Deut. 33:2–3), "host of heaven" (Isa. 40:26; Ps. 148:3). The parallelism in Job 38:7—morning stars: sons of God—suggests that the "sons of God" are symbolized as heavenly bodies (stars).

14. In the Neo-Babylonian period, courts were headed by officials called sartennu (the Chief Bailiff). In the Neo-Assyrian empire, the sartennu was a member of the state cabinet and traveled through the empire trying cases. See Ronald Westbrook, ed., *A History of Ancient Near Eastern Law*, 2 vols. (Leiden: Brill, 2003), 888–90, 919.

15. "The plan of salvation is calculated to make devils as well as Saints, for by and by we shall need some to serve as devils; and it takes almost as much knowledge to make a complete devil as it does to fit a man to go to the celestial kingdom of God and become an heir to His kingdom. . . . Neither you nor I would ever be prepared to be crowned in the celestial kingdom of our Father and our God, without devils in this world. Do you know that the Saints never could be prepared to receive the glory that is in reserve for them, without devils to help them to get it? Men and women never could be prepared to be judged and condemned out of their own mouths . . . without the power both of God and the devil. We are obliged to know and understand them, one as well as the other, in order to prepare us for the day that is coming, and for our exaltation. Some of you may think that this is a curious principle, but it is true. . . . We must know the evil in order to know the good. There must needs be an opposition in all things." Brigham Young, June 28, 1857, *Journal of Discourses*, 26 vols. (Liverpool and London: Latter-day Saints Book Depot, 1853–1886), 4:372–73.

to test humans and be a necessary adversary in a world where there must be opposition in all things.[16] As I now know, this is all that my satan was doing. The satan in my story points to a specific type of satan, an official in God's court but one who was not evil per se, or, given what you say, not yet evil. I say "yet" because we are so used to a linear story of creation and fall and redemption, but that it is not how it works. My satan points to a being of great power and responsibility; if that is used contrary to God's will, I think satan would become your Satan, the Great Dragon, evil. Anyway, enough of me. Tell me more about your Satan. He seems much more diabolical in your—what do you call it?—*New* Testament.

JOHN: Indeed, but remember, all such descriptions are but peerings through a dark glass, even when we see them first hand. You know this well. Yes, the New Testament, other early Christian writings, and some Jewish pseudepigrapha[17] offer a more devilish image of the Devil, which is why I was surprised at what you said. These descriptions depart to a degree from the emphasis of the ancient satans you have described, and stress the role of Satan—and let's here finally give him a proper name—as God's cosmic enemy and adversary of mankind in portrayals that depict him as the ruler of the world[18] and the prince of a host of evil spirits and demons.[19] This is the Dragon I saw.[20] There were many diabolical creatures in my vision, but he was chief among them.

JOB: Wherein is his rebellion? As I have said, my satan was not rebellious.

JOHN: Yes, I see that now. My Satan was once called Lucifer, the son of the morning, an angel.[21] The allegory of the garden explains his story and motivations.[22]

---

16. See Abraham 3:25 and 2 Nephi 2:27.

17. e.g., Wisdom 2:24.

18. Matthew 4:8–9.

19. Matthew 25:41.

20. See Revelation 12.

21. Doctrine and Covenants 76:25–26, 28; see also Isaiah 14:4–23, Revelation 12:3–9, Doctrine and Covenants 29:36–45, Abraham 3:27–28; cf. Daniel 8:10–12, Ezekiel 28:11–19, Luke 10:18, 2 Enoch, 29:4–5. See also Louis Ginzberg, ed., *The Legends of the Jews*, 7 vols., trans. Henrietta Szold and Paul Radin (Philadelphia: The Jewish Publication Society of America, 1909–1938; rpt., Baltimore: Johns Hopkins University Press, 1998), 1:62–64, 5:84–86 n. 35.

22. For further discussion, see Jeffrey R. Bradshaw and Ronan J. Head, "Mormonism's Satan and the Tree of Life," *Element* 4, no. 2 (2008): 1–52.

JOB: Ah yes, his tempting of Eve to eat the fruit of the tree of knowledge of good and evil. A good Hebrew story.

JOHN: Don't forget the tree of life, which was also forbidden.[23] My visions taught me many things. To eat the fruit of the tree of life and thus gain eternal life before passing through mortality was contrary to what God willed. This was rebellion, beyond Satan's purview! Now, our audience must be careful. This is a story, a myth. Do not get hung up on details—preterist, literalist, historicist, futurist: too many -ists! Let us simply say that the tree of life functions in the garden myth as a holy of holies that can only be approached by the pure. You find this idea in many ancient stories. As I have sensed it, Lucifer's intent was to have Adam and Eve fall into sin and then damn themselves by entering God's presence unprepared. It's a classic trope. As in your story I suppose he is there to test, but he goes beyond what God wanted. By introducing the fruit of the tree of knowledge to Adam and Eve the consequences of the Fall would come upon them, putting them in a position of vulnerability and danger.

JOB: And the danger was eating from the tree of life?

JOHN: Precisely! This was the great rebellion against God: to have them eat from the *tree of life in their sins.* Remember that the angel with the flaming sword was put there by God to guard the way to the tree *only once* Lucifer's rebellious plan was unveiled. In this story, his diabolical intent stands for a bigger principle, one which plays out in a myriad of other ways. In this universe, dark is as inevitable as light, but we are not to revel in it, to make it worse, to bend the darkness to our own glory, and to have it be dark everywhere and forever.

JOB: Why do you think he did this? Just because he is evil?

JOHN: The memory is dim, but don't you remember that Lucifer once claimed to us that he wanted to save all mankind? The garden reveals that it would have been in "unrighteousness and corruption,"[24] a damnable immortality that destroys the possibility of eternal life. This would have "destroyed the agency of man,"[25] not by attempting to compel people to

---

23. The Samaritan exegesis of Genesis 2:16 specifically excludes the tree of life from the original permission given to Adam and Eve to eat from the trees of the Garden.

24. Brigham Young, October 30, 1870, *Journal of Discourses*, 13:282.

25. Moses 4:3.

do right but rather by eliminating the possibility of a period of probation whereby individuals could exercise their free will. You know as well as I do that to be sinful and mortal is to be human. But to be sinful and immortal . . . well, that is hell, to be subject to his power. Life without death would have become meaningless and without hope and without hope we are listless and damned, with Lucifer our lord. That's what he wants and the story of his subversion in the garden symbolizes that.

JOB: I much prefer my satan to yours.

JOHN: But I think they must both be in there somehow. Don't you think?

The conversation continued, unreported. Then:

BOTH (turning to us): We think we have reached an understanding of the satans versus Satan. The satans are those entropic forces that pull at the fabric of unfolding novelty, but are necessary to it. The satans are the meteors that destroy dinosaurs, but open the world to mammals. The beauty of the world is conditioned by its opposite and that is simply the way of God's universe. To have purpose in such a world means to navigate constant and unrelenting attempts at destruction and desolation but with the hope we can create beauty. To triumph means to find that beauty. God calls us to join in the fray and create meaning. When the satans become Satan, it is only and forever entropy and darkness without meaning, worlds without end.[26] The satans are that which is done on all worlds and are necessary to them. The Satan is the enemy, the black hole that seeks to consume all of them.

---

26. These final sentiments are borrowed liberally from the mind of Steven L. Peck.

Alma and Abinadi:
The Worth of Souls

James D. Holt

In The Book of Mormon we read of the great prophet Abinadi who stood strong in his testimony in front of King Noah and his priests. One of those priests, Alma, "believed the words which Abinadi had spoken."[1] A common refrain among missionaries is that Abinadi, one of the greatest missionaries, only had one convert who he actually never knew had accepted the message. Would Abinadi be happy to know of Alma's conversion? What would they talk about?

* * * * * * *

ABINADI: I recognize you! You were among the priests of Noah who sat in judgment on me. You were one of those who was consecrated by Noah and supported in your laziness, idolatry, and whoredoms.

ALMA: I was. I sat and listened as you preached about the Ten Commandments and testified of the Christ who was to come.

ABINADI: You sat and listened?! You will have also heard many of the great truths that God has revealed to humanity; the redemption offered through Christ the Lord. You will also recall the condemnation and prophecy concerning your great king and those, like you, who supported him in his wickedness.

ALMA: I remember well the powerful testimony you bore of Christ the Lord, especially the message of redemption you preached. To hear the words as they came from your mouth, filled as they were with the spirit I could not

---

1. Mosiah 17:2.

deny the carnal nature that we as priests were exhibiting, similarly the hope that you gave when you told us that the law of Moses is only "a shadow of things to come," that it only pointed to Christ, and that we should teach them that redemption cometh through Christ the Lord, who is the very Eternal Father."[2] I felt condemned by my own sins. I do not, however, remember your words of prophecy and condemnation concerning the King and my friends; maybe because I only remember the self-condemnation I was experiencing as you spoke. You seemed to be speaking directly to me, and you stirred feelings that the others did not seem to share.

ABINADI: I am heartened that you remember my words so vividly, especially the feelings that they evoked within you. While I would not wish the condemnation that you felt upon anybody, it is only through a recognition of our carnal and devilish actions that we can hope to receive a forgiveness through the redemption of Christ. In comparison to the condemnation of God, my condemnation of the priests and King Noah would obviously pale in comparison. It is just a shame that you were unable to act upon your convictions and speak on my behalf.

ALMA: You misunderstand me Abinadi; though I understand why that might be the case. It is true that I never spoke in front of you of the inner turmoil I was going through and also the conviction that I felt. I do not understand why it was I among all the priests of King Noah that felt the way I did, or responded to the teachings in such a way to speak up for you and change my life. All I know is that for the longest time I had been troubled in my spirit as to the direction I was taking. I had begun "to wonder whether what [I] was doing was right or not. . . . [Your words and actions] began to sink more deeply into [my] soul that had done before. . . . [I] wondered whether the work of the Lord, if [I] were really engaged in it, would make [me] feel so restless and bitter."[3] In the midst of all of this I was emboldened by your words and your example.

When you returned to our city after being cast out, although you came in disguise the spirit of the Lord was unrestrained within you. You would not have noticed me but how I wondered when you began your declaration, "Thus has the Lord commanded me, saying—Abinadi, go

---

2. Mosiah 16:14–15.

3. David O. McKay, *Ancient Apostles* (Salt Lake City, Utah: Deseret Sunday School Union, 1918), 148–49. David O McKay used these words to describe Saul's feelings; similar feelings could also be imagined for Alma.

and prophesy among this my people."[4] You spoke with such power and conviction, that I dared hope that I was one of God's people. You were unashamed of the message you brought; it seemed to instill in you a confidence and a power that made our pretended power as priests and of King Noah be as nothing.

ABINADI: I remember well the events you describe. I came into the city in disguise, fully prepared to share the message that the Lord had given to me. I did not expect, however, to shed my disguise so quickly. I was horrified by what I saw and the spirit was unrestrained as I bore witness that God had sent me, Abinadi, to proclaim repentance to the kingdom.

You say that you were emboldened. What do you mean by this? I do not remember you declaring your conversion or speaking on my behalf.

ALMA: I felt sure you would have seen me. You finished speaking to the priests and King Noah; as you were being taken out I "believed the words which [you] had spoken, for [I] knew concerning the iniquity which [you] had spoken against [us]; therefore [I] began to plead with the king that he would not be angry with [you], but suffer that [you] might depart in peace."[5]

ABINADI: For that I am truly grateful. I do remember a commotion, but it was quickly subdued, and I was surrounded by the guards and led away. I had spoken the truth, and the comfort I felt from the Lord to know that I had spoken his words and delivered his message was joy enough for me. But to hear of the impact that these words had on you gladdens my heart. I only hope that you were able to live to express your devotion to the Lord.

ALMA: I do not know the reason why I was spared, maybe because of my previous loyalty to the King, or because of the guiding hand of the Lord. All I know is that I caused King Noah to be even more angry and he cast me out. In his anger he sent his servants after me to slay me; he had obviously had second thoughts about letting me live. I feel I may have made your situation worse however. Had it not been for my pleading the King may have been content to let you languish in prison. The conversion, or in his eyes defection, of one of his advisers could not have done your cause any good.

---

4. Mosiah 12:1.
5. Mosiah 17:2.

ABINADI: He left me in prison following your departure; as such I think
he had had time to begin to think rationally, though I'm not sure that he
ever had that capacity such was his manner. It now makes sense why you
do not remember my condemnation and prophecy of the priests for you
had been cast out. At the time I was brought back before him I gained
the impression that he was about to release me. I had warned him and
his priests that my words would "stand as a testimony against you. And
if you slay me ye will shed innocent blood, and this shall also stand as a
testimony against you at the last day."[6] I do not mean to suggest that Noah
had a spiritual awakening, or a rational thought, rather that I had shown
to him the consequences of his actions. The priests were ripe in their iniquity however, and they began to stir up Noah's anger against me so that
I would be put to death. They were perhaps emboldened by the thought
that this prophecy would only pertain to the king. But as they put me to
death I promised that the Lord would execute vengeance on those who
destroyed me. I was very clear to the priests about what I meant I promised that "even as ye have done into me, so shall it come to pass that thy
seed shall suffer the pains the I do suffer, even the pains of death by fire."[7]

Although this was far more condemnatory than I had ever been before, I was moved upon to declare these words. I did not know whether
this promise referred to their temporal sufferings or the sufferings of an
unrepentant soul as described by the prophets. Whichever is meant is in
the hands of God, and I know that I died with his name upon my lips
having fulfilled the work he had sent me to do.

ALMA: Oh my goodness, I had heard of this scene but to hear it described
by your lips really brings it home to me. How can you be so sure that you
had completed all of the work that the Lord had for you?

ABINADI: Do you not remember that at the beginning of my message
the priests attempted to take me? I assume they were planning my execu-
tion even then. I warned them: "Touch me not, for God would smite
[them] if [they lay their hands on me]."[8] As a result of this and the way in
which I spoke with the authority of God they saw that they had no power
to slay me until I had delivered my message. I recognized the hand of
the Lord as I declared to them: "I finish my message; and then it matters

---

6. Mosiah 17:9.
7. Mosiah 17:15.
8. Mosiah 13:3.

whither I should go, if it so be that I am saved."[9] How do I know that I had finished my work? I know because they would not have been able to kill me unless I had. While they may have imagined that I was referring to being saved from death; I know that I have been saved and exalted because of the redemption of our Lord Jesus Christ.

ALMA: My son shared a similar experience. He described witnessing the murder and martyrdom of many believers as he was asked by his companion, "Behold, perhaps they will burn us also. And Alma [my son] said: Be it according to the will of the Lord. But, behold, our work is not finished; therefore they burn us not."[10]

ABINADI: Your son showed great faith in the Lord. It heartens me to hear that you had a son who had such experiences and faith in the Lord; I wasn't ever sure why the Lord had called me to declare the message I did. I thought that perhaps it might have been to stand as a witness against Noah and his kingdom. He could not claim that he did not know the truth. In all honesty, while I accept the will of God, I hoped that this was not the only purpose of my words.

ALMA: While you may have felt that was the primary purpose of your message, as I look back over my life I recognize that that was only a small part of the work you had to do. You had so much more influence than just as a message against which others would be judged. Your words touched many. Indeed, so deep were they etched on my heart, that from the time of my exile up to when I heard of your death I hid myself and wrote all the words which you had spoken. You might wonder how I could remember your words in such detail. Never had I felt so inspired and guided than I did at that time; the Lord seemed to bring all of your words to my remembrance as I sat and wrote.[11]

ABINADI: My words had a great influence on you? I thought they had only been used to testify and condemn. To hear of their influence on you and your son gladdens my heart.

---

9. Mosiah 13:9.
10. Alma 14:12–13.
11. John 14:26.

ALMA: It is not just myself and my family. Following your death I was inspired to repent and to teach your words privately among the people of the city. I have to say that I was slightly better at staying hidden from the King than you had been; but then again your purpose was different from mine, and I never thought the disguise was very effective if you identified yourself loudly as Abinadi! Your preaching had touched many people, but they were afraid to go against the King. These people were receptive to the words that I taught. We found a place which was called Mormon where we gathered to teach and learn more of the Lord. On one day I was inspired to teach about repentance and then followed this up with baptism. I asked those who had gathered with me that if it was their desire to repent and follow the Lord "what have you against being baptized in the name of the Lord."[12]

One man called Helam was the first to volunteer to be baptized. Although I knew that I had been forgiven by God, I felt that as I baptized Helam I needed to be buried in the water as well to signify that I was beginning my covenants with the Lord afresh. You will be astonished to learn that over two hundred people were baptized that day.

ABINADI: That is astounding! But how could so many of you avoid being noticed by the king?

ALMA: The place of Mormon was on the borders of the land where no one ventured, so our activities were able to go unnoticed for a time. However, as you say it did come to the notice of the King. But through the providence and love of God we were warned that the King and his army were coming to destroy us and we were able to depart with our families into the wilderness.

I wish I could say that we found all to be well and our lives were easy as we found the rest of the Lord, but it was not. We were persecuted by Amulon (you will remember him) and also by the Lamanite king with whom Amulon had ingratiated himself. But through the Lord we were blessed that our burdens were made light and we were able to escape this burden to Zarahemla and be united with many of the people of Nephi who had held fast to faith in the Lord. There are many more events to narrate but please know Abinadi that your words were meant for far more than to testify of wickedness and be used as a judgment. They were a rebuke and an inspiration to me. Without your words and example there were many who would not have been brought to the knowledge of the truth.

12. Mosiah 18:10.

* * * * * * *

I end there because I have no idea how Abinadi could possibly respond to the knowledge that he had made such an impact on not just one man, but a nation. How must he feel when he sees the influence he continues to have today? It is interesting the path that this conversation took. How would Abinadi respond to one of the priests of Noah? He would have been forthright, but surely this would have been tempered by his testimony of the Lord. Some may feel that this conversation is a hagiographical dialogue that does little to draw out the tensions that may exist between Alma and Abinadi. Hopefully others will see the inner turmoil of Alma as he struggled to reconcile his faith as a priest of Noah with the message of Abinadi. Abinadi had always been my hero; his testimony and boldness always stood out. Perhaps Alma was behind him in my estimation because of his longevity and his assimilation (quite rightly) into the "establishment"; but these first events that occurred when he was a young man show him as a man with as great a faith and trust in the Lord as Abinadi. I was struck when writing this, though did not have time to explore it, how similar the conversion of Alma the Elder and Alma the Younger really were. The feelings that both must have felt are as Alma the Younger famously described it. His experience may be more graphically described than his father's, but if we overlook Alma the Elder and his conversion in favor of his son's, we miss the opportunity to explore the feelings that Alma the Elder must have felt as a father.

Tamar and David:
Personal Morality

Jason A. Kerr

On the surface, the stories of Tamar and Judah in Genesis 38 and the story of David and Bathsheba in 2 Samuel 11–13 look quite similar: a sexual act that shouldn't occur nevertheless occurs, and consequences follow. The consequences diverge, however: the story in Genesis, placed seemingly at random in the midst of the Joseph narrative, functions in part to explain Judah's change of heart that is crucial to the redemptive arc of the overall narrative. Tamar may dress as a prostitute to seduce her father-in-law Judah, but the effect is to bring him to recognize his own unrighteousness. David's story, though, brings a flood of death: Joab can't send Uriah into danger alone without the assassination becoming obvious, so eighteen more men have to die to cover David's sin. After the son born of his illicit coupling with Bathsheba dies, he allows the rape of his daughter Tamar (a story rife with allusions to the Genesis narrative) to go unpunished, which results in the death of his son and heir Amnon, and a brutal civil war against his son Absalom. What makes the justice of these two sexual acts so different? And, given that both of them factor explicitly into Matthew's genealogy of Jesus, what can these stories tell us about his identity and mission?[1]

---

1. In writing this I've consulted the commentaries on Genesis by E. A. Speiser (*The Anchor Bible: Genesis* [Garden City, N.Y.: Doubleday, 1964]) and Gerhard von Rad (*Genesis: A Commentary*, Rev. ed. [Philadelphia: Westminster, 1972]), the commentary on Samuel by Kyle McCarter (*The Anchor Bible: II Samuel* [Garden City, N.Y.: Doubleday, 1984]), and the annotated translations of both texts by Robert Alter (*The Five Books of Moses* [New York: Norton, 2008] and *Ancient Israel: The Former Prophets* [New York: Norton, 2014]).

* * * * * *

Tamar sits down to have a grandmotherly talk with her descendant, David. They're in the afterlife, but not the sort of afterlife where you suddenly understand everything that you missed in life. They have read the Bible, though, including the New Testament. They have to come to terms with their own histories—especially the justice or injustice of questionable sexual acts—but also with the place that Matthew gives them in the genealogy of Jesus. Tamar in particular seems to have wrestled with the writings of Paul. She was always a bit smarter than David, although apparently he found time to read the Church Fathers.

TAMAR: Well, son, here we are.

DAVID: Yes, grandmother. It's a bit awkward.

TAMAR: Our family history is . . . complicated, no?

DAVID: Let's be fair: people are mostly interested in your story because of mine. I founded a dynasty!

TAMAR: A dynasty that the prophets, from Samuel to Jeremiah, were mostly right to condemn!

DAVID: There's always Jesus.

TAMAR: Yes, because Jesus needed to come from a family whose need for salvation was so obvious and public!

DAVID: Who are you to lecture me? You slept with your father-in-law, dressed as a common whore! This family had problems long before I came along!

TAMAR: You may not think there's much difference between what I did with Judah and what you did with Bathsheba—and what you permitted to happen with your daughter Tamar—but there is. I took shame upon myself to save the family, but your shame nearly destroyed it.

DAVID: And yet the dynasty carried on!

TAMAR: Remember Nathan's parable, how the rich man took from the poor man? You are the rich man! In your youth, you had vigor, and you were always scrupulous to do the right thing, but once you got a little older . . . I don't know if you really were too old to go and join the siege of Rabbah, or if you just felt like you'd earned a break, or if the bureaucracy was starting to get so complicated that you just couldn't get away from Jerusalem, but there's nothing to justify sleeping all afternoon in the luxury of your own bed while your men were fighting in the spring heat, to say nothing of then raping one of their wives!

DAVID: And what's to justify sitting at the roadside, waiting to seduce your father-in-law? What makes you different from Bathsheba, there on her rooftop, wanting to be queen?

TAMAR: Judah needed a little help to see the value of family. Without me his line would have ended, and the reconciliation with Joseph might never have happened. We would have perished in the famine. You would not exist. You may not like it, but that's how it is.

DAVID: Then I was just keeping a venerable family tradition!

TAMAR: Except that your choices led to civil war with your son, Absalom. Your guilty conscience and your love for Amnon kept you from punishing where you ought to have punished. Injustice frequently falls on women, and we often have no means of redress. You were supposed to rule in justice, but there was no justice for Tamar. She brought healing and yet received shame! You let your injustice against both Bathsheba and Uriah put you aside from the true path. It's funny how so many questions of justice and injustice turn on one little organ—practically the scepter of lordship! Is there even any law besides that?

DAVID: But Bathsheba wanted—

TAMAR: You can tell yourself anything you want about her intentions, but you were still the king, a man in power, which hardly put her in a position to say no. Maybe after the rape she began to see ambition as a cover for shame. But you couldn't have known about any ambition in her when you started dreaming drowsily of afternoon delight! You couldn't even have known that when you had her husband killed! And all those messengers: you were always sending here and sending there. The entire court knew what you did almost before you had even finished. Even Uriah had to know: you made him stay on in the vain hope that he'd cover your deed, but that just gave all the servants you employed as your panders time to fill him in. You think he didn't know he was carrying his own death warrant? You think he didn't know that his every word and action condemned you?

DAVID: I paid for it. How I paid—

TAMAR: Sure, you felt bad when your children had to die: four for the one you killed, just like Nathan said—Bathsheba's son, Amnon, Tamar, and Absalom. Yes, you mourned, but they died for your sin, not you!

DAVID: I fasted and prayed seven days for Bathsheba's son, sleeping on the floor and refusing all comfort!

TAMAR: In that you simply did too late what Uriah did well when you tried to deceive him. It was part of your recompense.

DAVID: And so, I suppose, was Absalom's rebellion?

TAMAR: The king's justice had faltered. Vigilantism was the only way. It's never the best way, but sometimes it's the only way.

DAVID: I'm guessing that's how you will justify your own actions.

TAMAR: Judah had lost his way. Even though he had argued against killing Joseph, he still advocated selling him, and he participated in the deception against Jacob. Then he turned aside once again, from his own people to mine.

DAVID: He married his own Bathshua.[2]

TAMAR: Yes, and his sons with her were no good. Er was the firstborn—almost enough on its own to count against him among the patriarchs. Onan had learned from his father how to weasel out of being his brother's keeper. He made me feel like a whore, the way he used me for his pleasure while rejecting his duty. No, they cared neither for justice nor family.

---

2. Hebrew: "daughter of Shua"; see also 1 Chronicles 3:5.

DAVID: Say what you will, I loved my sons.

TAMAR: At the expense of your daughter! You did to her what Judah did to me: sent her away in her shame so you didn't have to think about it, refusing to acknowledge that your son failed in his duty toward her. And just as Joseph's torn and bloody coat [Hebrew: *ketonet passim*] ultimately testified against his brothers, so did Tamar's torn and bloody coat [Hebrew: *ketonet passim*] testify against you.

DAVID: Absalom's revenge was bitter payment for that.

TAMAR: No doubt, but it only served the outward form of justice. You were not transformed by it, not in your soul. Yes, you wept over the gate of the city when he was killed, but justice had slipped within you.

DAVID: For all my faults, I never whored myself the way you did.

TAMAR: Nonsense. You were worse than I was. Just as Nathan said to you, God had given you many of the daughters of Israel, and yet you lusted after another. Ingrate! There were women in your harem as abandoned as I was when I lived as a widow in my father's house, not even people, but objects you had forgotten to use, and yet you called Uriah's wife to your couch.

DAVID: But I was the king. I was the law, or so I thought.

TAMAR: Yes, that was your illusion. Law isn't the same as justice. What I did bent the law, perhaps, but it served justice.

DAVID: How is it at all just to sleep with your father-in-law?

TAMAR: He had forgotten about family. His selfishness about Shelah, his foolish presumption that the deaths of Er and Onan were my fault—he almost ended his line because of these thoughts. And then Bathshua died, while I still lived a forsaken widow, shamefully cast away and cut off, not belonging anywhere. I forgot family in the name of family.

DAVID: And when she died you saw your opportunity, because you had seen the ways of men.

TAMAR: That's the first candid thing you've said all morning. Yes, that was my opportunity. But Judah was trapped, too: he couldn't marry Shelah to anybody but me. He thought he was sparing his son from death, but alive like that he would have been the death of the line.

DAVID: Why does everything in our family happen at sheepshearing festivals?

TAMAR: Because the world turns upside down. People relax the usual rules, and sometimes that's what justice requires. You would not punish Amnon, so Absalom, as lord of misrule, took the part of a king.

DAVID: Judah wasn't planning on visiting a prostitute. He didn't bring anything to pay you with.

TAMAR: That's right. In this case justice required that I exploit his basic goodness a bit.

DAVID: Just like I did Uriah's.

TAMAR: To different ends, but yes.

DAVID: I got Uriah's wife; you got Judah's seal and staff, the marks of a man's power and standing—and the twins!

TAMAR: Ah, but I got them with the intent to reveal all. Your intent (once you had an intent beyond lust) was to conceal all. Which you then did badly, not only by using so many messengers, but once you brought Joab into it, eighteen more men had to die. You thought you could kill only one, but your ruthless general saw the reality more clearly.

DAVID: You're right: so much wrong cascaded from my choice.

TAMAR: Kings do stand above the law of their nations, but nobody stands above the law of God.

DAVID: How then did you escape the wrath? You prostituted yourself to your own father-in-law!

TAMAR: Sometimes you have to break the law to keep the law. Joseph may have been the son of the promise, but just as God affirmed the promise to Hagar and Ishmael, so too did it continue in Judah. His behavior threatened to end the line. It took a Canaanite woman to save this branch of Israel—your branch of Israel, and Jesus's branch, too. Everything about that seems wrong, and yet without it nothing would be right.

DAVID: What about the "temple prostitute" [Hebrew: *qedēsā*] thing? Was Hirah just trying to save face for his friend by not calling you a common harlot [Hebrew: *zōnā*], or were you engaging in some Canaanite cultic practice, sacrificing your chastity to the goddess of love?

TAMAR: Why does it matter?

DAVID: Because there's a difference between simply whoring and whoring after idols, like my son did.

TAMAR: Everything I did rests on ambiguity. Who knows what Judah thought he was doing? The place of the twin wells was better suited for a betrothal, as with his fathers, always meeting their wives at wells, and it wasn't a usual place to worship Astarte,[3] if you believe that sort of thing really happened.

DAVID: He was certainly unambiguous in condemning you!

TAMAR: I suppose we could argue about what was the nadir of his story: sleeping with me, or summarily condemning me to be burned without so much as calling for evidence.

DAVID: That is a hard case. By law we only burn people for the most blasphemous sexual crimes. I judged enough to know: Leviticus 20:16 instead of Leviticus 21:9.

TAMAR: That he presumed to judge me at all condemns him. He was claiming the part of a father with me—the very role he had been refusing to play. To say nothing about the double standard of his willingness to whore: if I ought to have burned, so should he.

---

3. A female deity worshipped by Canaanites.

DAVID: You acted the prophet with him, just like Nathan did with me. It can be difficult to get us men in power to see the injustice of our ways. You had to gamble pretty recklessly with your life in order to get him to do it.

TAMAR: Yes: how often do women die for the injustices committed by men? For us, justice can seem like a game of chance, but it was a game from which my soul would not let me abstain. I will admit to relishing the look on his face when he recognized his seal, though.

DAVID: Ah, so you're human after all?

TAMAR: I suppose so.

DAVID: I can see the justice in his admitting that you were more in the right than he.

TAMAR: He was more careful to do right by a prostitute he met in the road than by his own daughter-in-law—to say nothing of his own future descendants.

DAVID: But where is the redemption?

TAMAR: His whole story after the selling of Joseph had been one of turning aside—first to Canaan, and then to me at the place of the two wells. Admittedly he did well in at least persuading his brothers not to kill Joseph, but he was hardly in the right path. He was making his own law, just as you tried to do with Bathsheba and Uriah. That sort of autonomy is the pinnacle of pride and arrogance.

DAVID: So it was a big deal for him to acknowledge a law greater than himself, and to admit that you measured up to it better than he did?

TAMAR: Exactly.

DAVID: But I still can't reconcile your actions with justice. If what I did with Bathsheba was wrong—as I'm willing now to concede—how could it be more righteous than Judah's actions toward you?

TAMAR: Because he legally could have married me. By marriage I belonged to the family, but both of my husbands had died, and so had his wife. He could have given me to Shelah or taken me for himself. All I did was take the sovereignty into my own hands when he failed to act. And sovereigns do stand above the law, in the name of justice.

DAVID: So the problem with my sovereign seizure of Bathsheba isn't that I acted outside the law, but that I acted outside the law to do injustice?

TAMAR: Yes. I wasn't more just than Judah because I fulfilled some law better than he did, but because I used sovereignty more correctly. It's how you act outside the law that counts. What you do with your unconstrained freedom shows your character. You chose to become a "taker," just like Samuel predicted kings would be.

DAVID: I was always good at staying within the bounds of propriety so long as they obviously applied to me—as when I refused to strike Saul down—but once I stood above them, my mettle turned out to be less than I reckoned.

TAMAR: Nobody's mettle is all it could be. Fortunately, grace comes outside the law, too.

DAVID: I'm beginning to see how right it is that Jesus should descend from you. Like him, you emptied yourself in shame in order to save others. Part of his shame, I suppose, comes from me.

TAMAR: Yes, Matthew is so keen to have him descend from your line, to make him a king, but he gets a very mixed heritage from our family.

DAVID: From us he had to inherit the darkness he came to redeem.

TAMAR: That is why Matthew's genealogy also mentions Uriah's wife: to make your sins a part of Jesus's body. But Jesus also became like your Tamar: he came bearing the food of life, just like the hearty, healing dumplings that she cooked for Amnon, only to be put to shame.

DAVID: Like Gregory of Nazianzus wrote: what Jesus has not assumed he has not healed. Just like you took Judah's sin upon you and acted outside the law in order to put him on the path to reconcile with Joseph, ease Jacob's grief, and get our family the food we needed to go on.

TAMAR: Which created the need for a Moses, in time.

DAVID: Yes, the cycle of sin and redemption goes on. I redeemed the nation from Saul, but then I turned the wheel the other way. Solomon my son did the same, and the nation divided.

TAMAR: Matthew needed a Messiah who could be another Davidic king—everything you could and should have been—while also taking on and redeeming everything you failed to be.

DAVID: It's not that he needed my legacy to be the Messiah; it's that redeeming my legacy is what made him the Messiah.

TAMAR: He helps us see the bedrock of grace that's under everything. Even our follies rest on it, making it so that God can turn them toward our salvation.

DAVID: The same grace that redeemed Jesus's own illegitimacy, the sexual impropriety of his origins, which Joseph covered by adopting him at birth, and which God covered by adopting him at his baptism.

TAMAR: And Mary, who willingly and redemptively took sexual shame upon herself, playing her part in bending the arc of history back toward righteousness.

DAVID: Yes, Mary.

TAMAR: Perhaps you are learning, my son?

DAVID: Perhaps, my grandmother, perhaps.

Moses and Paul: The Law

Jared Ludlow

Moses is known as the great Lawgiver in the Judeo-Christian tradition. As part of the deliverance of the Israelites from Egypt, Moses led them to Mount Sinai for a rendezvous with deity. Later tradition traces the origin of what came to be called the "Law of Moses" to this dramatic experience at Sinai.

Over a millennium later, a Jew by the name of Paul (Saul) dramatically altered the way some Jews viewed this law. Sometimes referred to as a "radical Jew," Paul preached a freedom from the burden of the law which many later Christians interpreted as a complete cessation of previous commandments associated with Moses.

What would happen if these two pivotal scriptural figures met while Paul was preaching his interpretation of the law? Likely much of their dialogue would center on the law's efficacy or non-essentialness. Let's listen in and see what they might say about this crucial topic in relation to our salvation.

* * * * * *

MOSES: Paul, what did you do to my law; well, not my law, but the law given to me from the Lord? Do you not know that the Lord (Adonai) gave that law through me for his people's salvation?

PAUL: Yes, I know the Lord gave you that law. I can understand why you are frustrated, but believe me, I did not intend to unravel the law. In fact, I was one of its staunchest supporters in my early life. I studied the law of the fathers carefully with one of the best teachers of the law, Gamaliel.[1] I even zealously persecuted others for not observing it closely, but certain spiritual experiences changed my perspective on it.

---

1. See Acts 22:3.

MOSES: Spiritual experiences? Do you not know of the spiritual experience I had on Mount Sinai when the law was first revealed? Mount Sinai almost set on fire from the glory of the Lord! The voice of the trumpet sounded loud and long.[2] The finger of the Lord wrote out commandments for us to follow![3] Now that was a spiritual experience!

PAUL: Yes, I agree. That was an amazing experience with such glory that you had to veil your face from the people. But I was able to behold the risen Lord and that experience completely turned me around. However, the Jews continue to have a veil obscure their vision and understanding of the old covenant. Even when they read your words, Moses, the veil is upon their heart; but the veil is done away in Christ.[4] By the deeds of the law shall no flesh be justified because now the righteousness of God is manifested without the law, being witnessed by the law and the prophets.[5] The law helped guide our people for centuries, but it served its purpose and now God has a different plan for his children.

MOSES: A different plan for his children? There is only one plan: lead them to salvation. I taught the Lord's word that everyone who did the deeds and kept the statues of the law should live by them.[6] Wasn't the law given for their salvation?

PAUL: True, the law could lead them to salvation under certain conditions, but it was only a schoolmaster to bring us unto the Messiah.[7] It taught about and pointed to the salvific role of the Messiah. The Messiah has arrived, the law has been fulfilled, and faith has come so we are no longer under a schoolmaster but are children of God by faith in Christ Jesus.

MOSES: I know the Messiah came to earth. I visited with him on a mount as he was transfigured before me, but he kept the law, didn't he?

PAUL: You are right, the Messiah, Jesus, followed the law in his mortal life. His obedience to the law is part of the meaning of the law being ful-

---

2. Exodus 19:16–20.
3. Exodus 31:18.
4. See 2 Corinthians 3:13–15.
5. See Romans 3:21.
6. Leviticus 18:5.
7. See Galatians 3:24.

filled—he fulfilled or kept the law. But there is also a chronological aspect to the law where it was completed or finished.

MOSES: Well, when did that happen since Jesus observed the law throughout his life (with some disagreements from others on how to follow it)?

PAUL: In a way you could say he was a servant of the Jews to confirm the promises made unto the fathers,[8] but the law was completed with Jesus's death. His suffering for sin became the ultimate sacrifice for all God's children. His sacrifice ended the sacrifices of "your" law. He purchased us with his blood as he dictated the conditions of our salvation: to believe and have faith in him.

MOSES: Faith in the Messiah has always been important. Your associate Peter and others have clearly stated that I and all the prophets have proclaimed the coming of the Messiah and the necessity of faith in him.[9] How is this different?

PAUL: You had faith in he who was to come, but now that he has fulfilled his mission, he has taught us of a better way.

MOSES: A better way? Again, was not the law given through me adequate for the Israelites' salvation? We were commanded to take sacrificial animals, lay our hands on them, offer them to God, and sprinkle their blood for atonement. These were sin offerings to cleanse us from our impurities so that we could be in the presence of God. He promised us that if we were faithful to these commands, he would meet us at the tabernacle. His glory would sanctify us and the tabernacle so that he could dwell with us and be our God.[10]

PAUL: Yes, salvation could be gained through observing the law if done with the right intention: pointing towards the Messiah. The deeds of the law themselves could not bring salvation unless they were accompanied by the faith and understanding in how that salvation could be achieved. The blood of a sacrificial animal was only symbolic of the blood of Jesus's sac-

8. See Romans 15:8.
9. See John 5:45–47; Acts 3:22–25.
10. See Exodus 29:36–46.

rifice; of itself it had no salvific effect. Some sought salvation by the works of the law and faltered on the stumbling-stone: Jesus the Messiah.[11] But by sacrificing the animal and sprinkling the blood on the altar, one could strengthen their faith and understanding of God's power which brought the real cleansing and expiation.

MOSES: So are prohibitions against stealing, adultery, and bearing false witness still in force? Have God's moral standards changed?

PAUL: God forbid! God's moral standards are eternal, holy, just, and good. The unrighteous, such as those who get caught up in fornication, lasciviousness, hatred, drunkenness, and such things shall not inherit the kingdom of God.[12] Otherwise, we would become defiled with the desires and lusts of the flesh and lose the Spirit who can guide us on the path back to our Father. Furthermore, we are commanded to love one another, and the person who does so has fulfilled the law. The commandments to not commit adultery, not murder, not steal, not covet, as well as others are summed up in this one commandment: "love your neighbor as yourself." Love is the fulfillment of the law as we keep God's commandments.[13] Jesus taught: "He that hath my commandments, and keepeth them, he it is that loveth me: and he that loveth me shall be loved of my Father, and I will love him, and will manifest myself to him."[14]

MOSES: Well at least we can agree on this point: unrepentant sinners will not inherit the kingdom of God. But how will the people know which commandments to observe? For example, shouldn't we still keep the Sabbath day holy?

PAUL: If someone thinks that merely keeping the Sabbath day holy will bring salvation, then that person must be corrected. In and of itself, keeping the Sabbath day is not salvific; it is merely a shadow of things to come.[15] Jesus himself taught that he is Lord of the Sabbath, so we must center our faith on him.

---

11. See Romans 9:32; also Isaiah 8:13–15.
12. See 1 Corinthians 6:9; Galatians 5:16–21.
13. See Romans 13:8–10 and Galatians 5:14.
14. John 14:21.
15. See Colossians 2:16–17.

MOSES: But if you do not have the law, then anyone can achieve salvation, even Gentiles.

PAUL: Well not quite anyone; they need to accept Jesus as the Messiah or Savior, but part of Jesus's mission was to break down the barrier between Jew and Gentile so that all could participate in the covenants and promises given throughout the ages by God.

MOSES: The Lord gave those covenants and promises to the House of Israel! Are you saying they are for anyone now? The other nations were only there to provoke us to jealousy, to remember God.[16] God commanded us to become a peculiar people, a holy nation, and a kingdom of priests.[17] Why did we carefully separate ourselves from others while you're inviting the heathen to join with your fellow Jews? God sent his destroying angel before us to drive out the Hivite, the Canaanite, the Hittite, and others so that we could inherit the land without them.[18] Now you're saying the Gentiles can have inheritance with us in heaven above?

PAUL: You separated yourself from the nations so that you would not be defiled and led astray by their false religious notions, but through Christ the invitation is for all to become one in him: Jew and Gentile, male and female, bond and free.[19] The Gospel was indeed to go to the Jew first and then to the Gentile. But in his flesh, Christ abolished the law with its commandments and regulations. He wanted to reconcile both Jew and Gentile unto God in one body.[20] There are no longer strangers and foreigners, but fellowcitizens with the saints and members of God's household built on the foundation of the apostles and prophets with Jesus himself as the chief cornerstone.[21] God is not the God of the Jews only, but also of the Gentiles.[22]

MOSES: It seems, then, there is no longer a place for Israel as God's covenant people. Who are God's covenant people?

---

16. See Deuteronomy 32:21.
17. See Exodus 19:5–6.
18. See Exodus 23:20–33.
19. See Galatians 3:28.
20. See Ephesians 2:14–16.
21. See Ephesians 2:19–20.
22. See Romans 3:29.

PAUL: God has not forgotten his people, Israel, and especially the promises and covenants made to them through the prophets. To the Israelites belong the election, the glory, the covenants, the receiving of the law, the temple worship, the patriarchs, and the promises. However, lineage from Abraham is not enough to be the true seed of Abraham.[23] One is not a Jew or a covenant person who is merely one outwardly. One has to be a covenant person inwardly. Circumcision is now of the heart, in the spirit, and not in the letter.[24] Because Abraham was deemed righteous and granted promises of eternal inheritance through his faith without circumcision, he will be father also of those who walk in the steps of that faith.[25] God will justify both the circumcision by faith and the uncircumcision through faith. Does that void the law through faith? God forbid: we establish the law.[26]

MOSES: So what's the role of the house of Israel now?

PAUL: The house of Israel continues to play an important role since they had the oracles of God committed unto them. God has preserved a remnant through whom he will do his work. The others have been blinded and their stumbling has made it possible for salvation to come to the Gentiles who can then provoke them to jealousy, to return to God. Some of the branches of the true tree have been broken off, but others remain. Meanwhile, some of the wild branches have been grafted in among them to partake of the root and fatness of the true olive tree. Any who turn to God by accepting Jesus as the Deliverer can be grafted or re-grafted into the tree. This state of affairs will continue until the fulness of the Gentiles shall come in and then all true Israel shall be saved.[27] The Israelites are still beloved for the fathers' sakes, and it is my heart's desire and prayer to God that Israel might be saved.[28]

MOSES: This new situation will create a large and diverse community. You will surely feel like you need to do everything yourself to maintain the congregations you helped found as well as appease longer-term members

---

23. See Romans 9:7–8.
24. See Romans 2:29.
25. See Romans 4:11–12.
26. See Romans 3:30–31.
27. See Romans 11:16–28.
28. See Romans 10:1.

from a Jewish background. I can speak from experience that it is too much to try to do everything yourself. My father-in-law, Jethro, helped me to understand the importance of organization and delegation. I chose able men out of Israel and organized them to be good examples to the people and judge them in small matters related to the law.[29] I would encourage you to value the assistance of others and rely on their experience and efforts to spread the work.

PAUL: That is great advice. I have had a few disagreements with my fellow workers when we did not see eye-to-eye. You're right, I should not try to do everything myself and I probably need to humble myself towards my co-workers in the service of the Lord. In my letters I do try to thank those who have sacrificed so much for Christ, but sometimes I let my notion of who is properly following the Lord's covenants lead to passionate disputes.

MOSES: Covenants are at the heart of our relationship to God. What an amazing blessing that he has condescended to enter into covenant relationships with us, his children. Do not let your listeners lose sight of the fact that their faith and baptism is leading them into a covenant relationship. But beware on how you dictate to others their obedience or non-obedience; it may not always be your place to declare their righteousness. I myself tried to strongly enforce who it was that was obedient to the covenant, but I was not always obedient myself, yet the Lord was merciful and allowed me to see the Promised Land even if I could not enter it. Maybe it is the Spirit of the Lord that manifests who is a covenant person today and determines what their status is before God.

PAUL: I agree, the Spirit of the Lord is key in all that we're trying to do. Truly anyone can be adopted or incorporated into the family of God to receive all the blessings and glory he has reserved for his children because the Spirit itself bears witness with our spirit that we are children of God. And if children, then heirs of God and joint-heirs with Christ.[30] I have been ministering the gospel among the Gentiles, as a minister of the new testament or covenant, so that their offering might be acceptable and sanctified by the Holy Ghost.[31]

---

29. Exodus 18:24–26.
30. See Romans 8:16–17.
31. Romans 15:16.

MOSES: As you have explained, Paul, though the manner of worship may have changed, the demand for one's heart has not. I suppose anyone with a willing heart can bring that as an offering to the Lord and he will recognize their love and obedience and reward it.

PAUL: Amen! Praise be to God for the gift of his Son who has shown us a more excellent way!

* * * * * * *

Obviously this is a fictitious dialogue, but it discusses some of the issues that are commonly raised in discussions of Pauline theology in relation to the Law of Moses. Paul and his contemporary Jews had become heavily entrenched in the Law of Moses to the point where it seems most had lost the perspective of its symbolic relationship to the future messianic mission. When Paul began focusing his missionary efforts on the Gentiles, it created tensions in the early church as some Christians wanted to maintain aspects of the Law of Moses while others were ready to be free from the burden of the law. Paul fought vociferously for the view that one need not become a good "Jew" in order to become a good "Christian."

Paul and other early Christian leaders viewed Jesus as the fulfillment of many earlier (Old Testament) prophecies. They even saw the Law of Moses as a source for prophetic knowledge about Jesus's future mission. Jesus himself testified to his disciples following his resurrection: "These are the words which I spake unto you, while I was yet with you, that *all things must be fulfilled, which were written in the law of Moses,* and in the prophets, and in the psalms, *concerning me.*"[32] Unfortunately, much of the clear perspective of Moses towards the future Messiah is lacking from the Hebrew Bible (excepting some references such as Deuteronomy 18:15–19), but early Christians did not shy from saying that he knew of Jesus's important salvific role. Philip told Nathanael that they had found the one "of whom *Moses in the law,* and the prophets, did write, Jesus of Nazareth, the son of Joseph."[33] In one confrontation with antagonists, Jesus declared that Moses would judge them, "for had ye believed Moses, ye would have believed me: for he wrote of me."[34] Thus it seems Moses

---

32. Luke 24:44; emphasis added.
33. John 1:45; emphasis added.
34. John 5:46.

understood Jesus's future mission better than a current reading of the Old Testament lets on, so he probably would not have been as surprised by Paul's radical modification of the law as portrayed above.

Paul became the pivotal figure in the transition between what came to be called Judaism and Christianity. Yet Paul never intended to create a new theology or religion, even after his overwhelming experience on the road to Damascus led him to believe in Christ and his fulfillment of earlier law and prophecy. Paul was simply a Jew who had now accepted Jesus as the Messiah, but his work as the "apostle to the Gentiles" changed everything. The role of the Law of Moses was fundamentally transformed. Paul's emphasis was on what changed him: belief in Jesus as the promised Messiah and the risen Lord. Paul testified that the figure leading the Israelites throughout their history was none other than Jesus; Christ was the Rock from which the Israelites drank.[35] Even while imprisoned and with death looming over him, Paul indefatigably preached Jesus from the Old Testament as Acts 28:23 bears witness: "there came many to him into his lodging; to whom he expounded and testified the kingdom of God, persuading them concerning Jesus, both out of the Law of Moses, and out of the prophets, from morning till evening."

Paul's message was that whether Jew or Gentile, Jesus Christ was the path to salvation, not the Law of Moses. Paul did not invalidate the past Law of Moses, but warned of misunderstanding its future role. The Law of Moses had served as the key vehicle for the covenant relationship between God and his people. Now that Christ had come, his teachings and atonement became the basis for a covenant relationship with God. For Paul, the eternal answer became Jesus.

---

35. See 1 Corinthians 10:4.

Abraham and Thomas: Doubt

Steven L. Peck

A dreary plain stretches from horizon to horizon. The sun is just beginning to dip below the descending hills far away. Low, thorny shrubs crawl woody and brittle from the dry, parched ground in scattered patches, their leaves dun colored and miserly-thick to retain moisture. An old well with a shallow stone wall stands conspicuously alone in the desolation, suggesting a center place to the emptiness. On a rock sits a white-bearded man. His hands and face match the land. His blue robe speaks of pastoral desert wealth and power. On his fingers glimmer silver rings with auspicious gems of various hues and quiet luster, announcing his importance. From the south a wanderer approaches—a young man with a close-cropped beard and hair shorn Roman style. A traveler's wallet bounces empty on his hip. He approaches the older man.

ABRAHAM: Greetings.

THOMAS: Greetings.

ABRAHAM: May I draw you some water?

THOMAS: I am grateful, Sir. I am parched and weary.

The old man lowers a bucket and brings up sloshing, cold water. With an ancient gourd dipper, he takes an offering from the wooden pail and hands it brimming to the younger man who drinks it messily, slaking his thirst aggressively.

THOMAS: What a strange place. I don't know how we came here, but I know you—Father Abraham.

The older man nods and likewise takes a drink, avoiding the younger man's gaze.

THOMAS: And you know me.

Abraham nods, somewhat curtly.

ABRAHAM: The Doubter.

The Younger man smiles.

THOMAS: I prefer Thomas.

ABRAHAM: I do not remember how I came here.

THOMAS: Nor I. Yet I know who I am. I remember my life. And I know who you are, but I know only what I've learned of you from the scriptures. How strange. You are like a story come to life but without the fullness gained in really knowing a person.

The old man nods.

ABRAHAM: It is the same.

THOMAS: Father Abraham. Whatever brings us together, it is an honor. You have been an example and hero to me throughout my life. The father ancestor of us all. I have bragged my whole life I am the seed of Abraham—of your seed! Even the deity identifies Himself as the God of Abraham. The Friend of God you are called!

The younger man bows low. The older man considers the younger man then nods and motions to the ample rock upon which he is sitting. The young man accepts and sits, somewhat stiffly, beside Abraham.

ABRAHAM: And you. You yourself. You walked with He whom we all worship. Yet I know only that you refused the testimony of your fellows when he returned as promised. How is that possible? You who walked with him? How is it you doubted?

The younger man is silent for a while. Then staring into the wilderness he speaks.

THOMAS: I knew him well. "Master," we called him. Our "Teacher." We walked miles together and had many conversations. Of lilies and foxes. Of land and seas. Of the future, yet things were never as clear then as they were in retrospect. Looking back I can read the portend of his words that we missed when he spoke them. He talked to us in parables at times so enigmatic and puzzling that they seemed but nonsense children's stories. At others he spoke with such clarity that there was little question whereof he spoke. Still we trusted that he was the one who would bring the Kingdom of God.

ABRAHAM: Yet in the end you doubted?

THOMAS: In the end? Neither his death nor resurrection was ever an end. And we doubted before and after. Do you not doubt? Ever? You knight of faith. Is it so easy for you never to doubt?

The older man lowers his gaze, seems about to answer, then after a small, almost imperceptible shudder asks his companion another question.

ABRAHAM: How did you bear it? Being chastised by God's Son for your failure of belief? How did you keep from hiding under the rocks?

THOMAS: He did not condemn me.

ABRAHAM: Did He not single you out and say, "because thou hast seen me, thou hast believed: blessed are they that have not seen, and yet have believed"? You alone of the apostles was so chastised.

THOMAS: No, they had believed no more than I. Do not forget that he had appeared to Mary and the other women who followed him. They told the other apostles so, and neither did Peter nor the others believe them. And even the women thought he was dead. Only when he appeared were their doubts set aside. As I said, we all doubted then. We doubted after. I have wandered in the East in far and strange India, and sometimes it all appears to me as a great story of magic and enchantment told by campfire light under the stars that in the day seems easily dismissed. Doubts must be present for faith to act. It is my doubts that allow my faith to flower. Courage is not courage unless fear is present. Without fear, courage is impossible—for it is just a rash act otherwise, and there is nothing praiseworthy about it. It is the fear that gives rise to the possibility of courage. So with faith. Without doubt, faith is a blindness. An undeserved and callow confidence.

ABRAHAM: But he said, "Blessed are those who have not seen, and yet have believed." Not seeing is central to faith! Not seeing defines the blindness you seemingly condemn. Doubt is to be resisted. Set aside.

Thomas shakes his head.

THOMAS: No. Doubt cannot be resisted or set aside. It is always there. It is a companion that must be invited to the conversation, "Blessed are they that have not seen, and yet have believed." The weight is on the "yet" in that scripture. The decision lies in the "yet." The not seeing is not something that ever goes away. It cannot be resisted or set aside. It is a condition we can only confront with "yet." Do you disagree? I speak foolishly perhaps. You are the father of faith. You had so much faith you are called the Friend of God. Yet, forgive the question of a man, called the "Doubter." For your story . . . the Akedah. I do not understand it. Can you tell me? I have the scripture, but it seems . . . something is missing and . . .

Thomas trails off. Abraham sighs and one by one starts to pull the rings from his fingers and lay them on the rock beside him.

ABRAHAM: Friend of God. Yes. It was "accounted to me for righteousness." Yes. And yet . . . (*His voice shakes.*) Have you ever wondered if I failed the test?

THOMAS: No. That isn't true. Everyone knows your story. You . . .

ABRAHAM: No. Hear me, friend. Perhaps I failed. Your own words condemn me.

THOMAS: How can that be?

The older man rises from the rock and walks to the well and, peering into its depths, starts to speak.

ABRAHAM: As you said, I failed to doubt. I pushed it away. I tried to do the easy thing and in so doing failed to have faith.

THOMAS: Surely killing Isaac was not the "easy thing."

ABRAHAM: No. No easy thing that. But easier than challenging God. Challenging, "The God of Abraham." (*He gives a short ironic laugh.*)

Abraham turns around and walks back to the rock. He looks over the top of Thomas and into the desolate landscape.

ABRAHAM: The wilderness goes on and on here. It does not seem to end. What a strange place. Perhaps this is just the place to tell the real story. To make the events clear. It has been a while.

Thomas stands, leads the older man back to the rock, and helps him resume his seat.

THOMAS: So the scripture is in error?

ABRAHAM: In error? In no ways that matter. But it is incomplete. Here. Attend. (*He turns to Thomas.*) Yes. It was late on a moonless night, and the stars were bright and glorious outside my tent. Sariah was sleeping; the lad was not far away, talking in his sleep as he was wont to do. I stepped out to see the great lights scattered through the heavens that I so loved. As I stared at the sky, a familiar voice said, "Abraham," and as I had answered many times before I said, "Here I am."

THOMAS: This is the story that has so moved me.

ABRAHAM: Then you know the words of terror that followed: "Take your son, your only son Isaac, whom you love, and go to the land of Moriah, and offer him there as a burnt offering on one of the mountains of which I shall tell you."

THOMAS: What did you say?

ABRAHAM: I said nothing.

THOMAS: Yet you had argued for the saving of Sodom and Gomorrah, why not your son?

The old man shakes his head in sorrow and speaks again, more to himself than to the young man.

ABRAHAM: Why did I not argue? Why did I not demand reasons from God? Was I trying to be like Father Adam and make a sacrifice for which I could answer only, "I know not," when asked why he did it?

THOMAS: And how did you know it was God? Maybe it was the voices that come from the night when one first awakes. That chatter of a groggy soul that means nothing.

ABRAHAM: No. It was clear at the time. Or so it felt. But after, as I walked through the dry landscape with Isaac to Moriah, it seemed uncertain. I doubted. But I pushed it aside. I refused its presence.

The young man looks at the older man and places a tentative hand on his shoulder.

THOMAS: Did you tell Sariah?

ABRAHAM: How could I? But she knew. She kept asking me, where is the sacrificial animal? She knew we would not find one on the way. She knew me well enough, unlike the boy, that I was upset beyond reckoning. She saw the fear in my eyes. She recognized the certainty of purpose that undergirds some hard and awful task. She suspected. She saw in me both my refusal of doubt and my resolve. Since the day the miraculous boy was born, she feared for him. And as she looked into my eyes, she sensed that her greatest fear was about to be visited upon her. She did not understand its form, motive, or context but she could feel doom impending like the dark black storm clouds of the late summer that bring the flash floods and tearing winds. She begged me to stay. She demanded the lad stay behind. He wept as early in the morning of the next day I loaded the ass with wood for the sacrifice and supplies for a few days. But in the end we departed.

THOMAS: You were so certain.

ABRAHAM: Yes. Even as the boy asked where the sacrifice was and I lied and said God would provide one. I did not allow myself to doubt.

THOMAS: This is what I have never understood. Is not God bound by law? Is he not the guarantor of the very rules that bind the universe? How can even he ask this thing of you?

ABRAHAM: Only if he is higher than all law.

THOMAS: But he is not. Am I wrong?

ABRAHAM: No. You say you do not understand. Neither did I. But then I was known far and wide for my obedience to God! All my people. All those who knew me understood that I obeyed God well. I was not acting for myself. I delivered my tithes to Melchizedek faithfully. I obeyed in all things.

THOMAS: So you did it for the expectations of others.

ABRAHAM: No. You do not understand. It was how I saw myself as well. Their perception of me was because I had cultivated that, because I believed it too. I obeyed in all things. All things! And that was the test! (*He weeps.*) God was testing me to see if I would obey Him even against higher things. Those things that He Himself honored and loved. Which mattered more? The principles of love by which He ruled or Him the person who dwelt above?

THOMAS: So you bound your son.

ABRAHAM: Yes.

THOMAS: And you raised the knife.

ABRAHAM: Yes.

THOMAS: And an angel stopped you.

ABRAHAM: Yes. (*His words are broken and interrupted by sobs.*) As I raised the knife to thrust it into the waiting throat of my beloved son, a hand with the grip of a thousand men closed around my fist and held it steady and sure and stopped the blade's descent. Then a voice sweet and familiar whispered in my ear, "Do not lay your hand on the lad or do any harm to him." And I looked at the angel in surprise, in fear. For of truth it was an angel[1] and of truth it was Sariah.[2] She had followed us. I dropped the knife and embraced her. She looked at me and said, "I know you fear God, since you have not withheld your son. But this is not His will, my husband. As his mother I too have a say in this matter. Come. I've brought a proper sacrifice." And I looked to a thicket where she had tied a lamb without blemish.

The younger man wraps an arm around the weeping patriarch. The older man has a far-away look in his eyes.

THOMAS: How strange. I had always held your actions as a type of my Savior's sacrifice. It does not seem to fit in the story you tell.

The old man dries his eyes, staring hard at the younger man

ABRAHAM: Does not fit? I think you are wrong. Are we all not bound by sin just as my son was on the altar? His was no free act I assure you, just as we are constrained and roped by sin through no desire of our own. Is not the delivery of the lamb by an act of love a better metaphor for what the Redeemer did? To put me as a type of the Father makes of him a monster

---

1. In the earliest manuscripts of the Akedah no angel appears and Abraham sacrifices his son, see Omri Boehm, *The Binding of Isaac: A Religious Model of Disobedience* (New York: T & T Clark, 2007), 20–33.

2. The commentaries on the Akedah (the binding) are extensive. In Jewish, Christian, Islamic, and philosophical sources. The angel has received a lot of attention, as has Sarah's reaction, especially in literature, including Soren Kierkegaard's *Fear and Trembling* (1843), Dan Simmon's *Hyperion* (New York: Broadway Books, 1989), and Mary Rakow's *This is Why I Came* (Berkeley: Counterpoint, 2015). For my own interpretation of the Akedah, I drew on these sources and others, but for a particularly "Mormon" reading I drew on Jeffery R. Holland's 2008 October General Conference talk, "The Ministry of Angels," in which he says, "we are reminded that not all angels are from the other side of the veil. Some of them we walk with and talk with—here, now, every day. Some of them reside in our own neighborhoods. Some of them gave birth to us, and in my case, one of them consented to marry me" (available at https://www.lds.org/general-conference/2008/10/the-ministry-of-angels). These kinds of angels are well known to me, and the only kind I've ever had dealings with. That Sarah was the angel in the Akedah seems as good a possibility as those I've seen in the commentaries.

who acts against all higher laws for arbitrary acts of horror and control. No, love must be the primary attribute of all things related to our Redeemer.

THOMAS: Redeemer. Yes.

ABRAHAM: That is why it was accounted unto me for righteousness, for I too was in need of redemption and atonement. I was redeemed. And in Him much is accounted for righteousness that would not otherwise be so. Do you understand? Do you understand that I am the Friend of God not because I foolishly did not question some interpretation of his call and words or because I came to see in certainty where doubt would have served better? I was about to murder my son! I am the Friend of God because I accepted the lamb tied in the thicket. An act of love.

THOMAS: Yes. (*Laughing.*) You make my own argument about doubt better than I.

ABRAHAM: That was my last sacrifice. That lamb. After, I could no longer look at the bronze knife that had spilled so much blood. There was a change.

THOMAS: That change I understand.

ABRAHAM: Of that I have no doubt.

And at Abraham's words they laughed together long and merrily. Then the two disciples talked deep into the strange and lonely night about life, its meaning, and how it is best lived in the presence of faith and doubt and love.

Mark and Luke: Women's Roles

Julie M. Smith

MARK: Could you ever have imagined this?

LUKE: No, no, of course not. I expected Theophilus to read it and maybe share it with a few people. And I suppose if I'd thought about it, it might have occurred to me that some of those people might share it with a few other people. But for it to become scripture? To be known around the world? Still read two thousand years later? Never, never could I have imagined that. Do you know that there are people who earn their livelihood for their entire lifetime studying just your book?

MARK: Yes, I heard about that, and it amazes me. Of course, my situation was a little different than yours: I was mostly just writing down a story that many storytellers were already telling. But I never thought the written version would be of much significance. I never even imagined it. You know what else I couldn't have fathomed?

LUKE: What?

MARK: That you'd be the one whose gospel was thought to be the most woman-friendly!

LUKE: What? Why? My gospel is very positive about our sister disciples! Some of those who studied my work closely noted that of the material I have that isn't found in any other gospel, a disproportionate amount concerns women. And did you know that Mary was one of my sources?

MARK: I had suspected she was. And it was a good thing indeed that her reminisces were incorporated by you into the record: if you hadn't done that, her precious witness would have been lost in the sands of history. A sad fate, and one—as you well know—all too common for the testimony of women.

LUKE: Yes, indeed. And I was happy to do it. But how then do you not think my gospel is friendly to women? I went out of my way when I was writing to be sure women were included. You do know that I would regularly take a man's story and a woman's story and tell them both, precisely to make the point that the gospel is relevant to both men and women? I did it with background material, like Mary's praise song and Zechariah's praise song. I did it with Jesus's parables, like the lost sheep and the lost coin. I did it with miracles—telling one story about a man healed on the Sabbath and another of a woman healed on the Sabbath. I paired stories like this over a dozen times! One of those pairs even compares female disciples to male disciples. That's welcoming to women, isn't it?

MARK: Well, yes, in a sense, I suppose. But it also emphasizes that women are different—other than. That can develop into a problem of not seeing women as equal, especially since everything you wrote has a tendency to show women in traditionally female roles.

LUKE: Right. That's a good thing.

MARK: No, it isn't a good thing! Why didn't you show women in roles that had been restricted to men?

LUKE: Well, I did to an extent. I showed the female disciples as financial backers of Jesus's ministry.

MARK: Well, yes, there was that. I suppose I need to give you a bit of credit for that. But women spending money is hardly revolutionary—it could actually be said to feed a stereotype. My criticism is that you don't show women exercising the full privileges that the gospel gives them to break out of some of the restrictions that tradition had placed on them.

LUKE: I did, though. I'm the only one of the four of us who included the story of the time when a woman praised Mary by saying that her body was blessed for bearing Jesus, and Jesus gently corrected her by pointing out that the real blessings are for those who hear the word of God and follow it.

MARK: Well, yes, that's another minor instance. But it's no secret that a lot of your text copies my text and—

LUKE: Does that bother you?

MARK: In general, no. Not at all. I inherited the tradition as well. But what does bother me are some of the changes that you made to my text. It's as if you weren't comfortable with the implications of some of the stories that I told about women, and you felt the need to clean things up—to, if I may be so bold, censor some of the record.

LUKE: Like what?

MARK: Well, why did you omit the story of the Greek woman who demanded an exorcism for her daughter?

LUKE: Well, there were several reasons for that . . .

MARK: Was one of them that you were uncomfortable with the idea of a woman debating with Jesus—and winning?

LUKE: Well, there were other reasons at play. . . . I did, after all, omit that entire section—not just that one story. But I have to admit that I worried that that story would give people the wrong impression of Jesus.

MARK: What, the impression that he listened to women?

LUKE: That's not fair. Of course he listened to women, and of course that's a good thing. But you made it sound as if she changed his mind.

MARK: She did.

LUKE: How could she change the mind of the Savior of the world?

MARK: How could the Savior of the world model how to be humble and teachable if he never changed his mind?

LUKE: Well, that's an interesting way of looking at it! We'll need to discuss that topic at length some other time! But aren't you making too big of a matter over this? There are other reasons that I left out that particular story.

MARK: OK, but it isn't just about that one story. Many of the stories which you include—the ones you are lauded for because they mention women—show women in traditionally female roles. Elisabeth has a baby. Mary has a baby. A widow serves in the temple. Another widow has her son restored to life. A woman anoints Jesus's feet. A woman sweeps her house in a parable. It seems like all of your unique material about women shows them in stereotypical roles. Was there *nothing* in our culture and its treatment of women that you thought needed to be challenged by the gospel?

LUKE: Of course, of course there were things. And I addressed them. I even went so far as to criticize the apostles for thinking that the female disciples' resurrection witness was nothing but an idle tale!

MARK: OK, I suppose you deserve some credit for that.

LUKE: And did I not mention that Anna was a prophet awaiting the Messiah? I believe I am the only one of us who included her story. She's really the first one to share the good news—the first missionary. I told of Mary and Martha in a story than emphasized discipleship and learning over domestic chores. But you are nonetheless right that, in general, I thought it was important to show women doing the kinds of things that women normally do: taking care of children and that sort of thing.

MARK: That's precisely my complaint!

LUKE: But why are you complaining about that? Women did these things. Women have always done these things. Women will continue to do these things. Should we not honor that work? Should we not teach others that it is honorable and important work? I included—and you did not—Jesus comparing himself to a mother hen. That's how you honor women: by showing that what they do is honorable!

MARK: Well, yes, of course, but—

LUKE: That's all I was doing. I was honoring the roles that women have always and will always fill by showing how the good news honors women in those roles.

MARK: Yes, but don't you see how that leaves the impression with your readers that those are the only roles that are acceptable for women?

LUKE: But I never say that. I even make some moves in the opposite direction, as I mentioned.

MARK: Yes, but it still creates that impression. That's why I thought it was so important to show women in other roles—the kinds of roles which men normally occupy.

LUKE: Isn't it a problem for you if the only way to honor women is to try to make them into men?

MARK: Now, don't put words in my mouth. I didn't try to make women into men. I just showed women in men's roles sometimes.

LUKE: Like that anointing story you tell?

MARK: That's a very important story to talk about—and part of my complaint against you. That story is the hinge of the entire good news, really. It clearly explains what it means when we say that Jesus is the Anointed One. And it is no accident that it is a woman who anoints him! That's a good example of allowing women to occupy roles that our traditions say are not for them. Why didn't you emphasize this point in your telling of Jesus's story? Why did you omit this story from your record?

LUKE: Well, I'd already told an anointing story.

MARK: Actually, I've always been confused on that point: is the story you tell another version—a very watered-down version, I might note—of the same story that I tell, or was that a separate incident? Do you know?

LUKE: Look, Mark, that isn't really the point, is it?

MARK: Well, I suppose it isn't. But let's just say that when you look at both of our gospels, it is glaringly obvious that at the beginning of the story of Jesus's death, you are following me word for word—

LUKE: But I thought you said—

MARK: I don't have a problem with the word-for-word part. What I have a problem with is that you obviously censor my anointing story. Why? You are clearly following me, but then you leave it out. It's the most important story in the whole good news! I cannot imagine why you would leave that out!

LUKE: I don't like the word "censor." I left it out for a variety of reasons.

MARK: One of which is how it portrayed the woman?

LUKE: Well, yes. Again, I didn't want to give people the wrong idea—the idea that Jesus was subservient to that woman. Or subservient to anyone, really.

MARK: Again, this is the same principle as with the Greek woman's story: How can Jesus model humility—how can he teach what it means to be a disciple—if he never receives from anyone? And of course it hammers the message home all the more when it is a woman who anoints him.

LUKE: Yes, I see your point. But how many women will have the opportunity to anoint Jesus's head?

MARK: Exactly one, I think.

LUKE: Precisely. And how many women will bear and raise children?

MARK: Most of them, I suppose.

LUKE: So then do you not see the value in showing the honor inherent in the kinds of things that most women spend most of their lives doing?

MARK: Yes, I do, but not at the cost of restricting women's spheres just because that is what has traditionally been done.

LUKE: I've said nothing about tradition. I have no desire to simply support or undermine our traditions or anyone else's. I was just very focused on being sure that women's daily lives were reflected in my text and that they felt included and honored. I wanted women—and men!—to know that in the kingdom, women's work is considered honorable.

MARK: Which is a good thing. But why did you have to omit everything I included that showed an expansion of women's spheres?

LUKE: Well, I didn't omit everything like that—I kept the story of the menstruating woman.

Both Mark and Luke shudder a bit.

MARK: Indeed you did. A story I myself was hesitant to include given its . . . ah . . . topic. But it was clear to me that that incident was important to understanding Jesus's ministry and it was even clearer to me that the female listeners and storytellers found it greatly important. So I included it.

LUKE: Exactly my thinking! And I kept your story almost exactly as I found it . . . just perhaps polishing the wording a bit.

MARK: I'll ignore your criticism of my writing style for now, but your hoity-toity approach will need to be the topic of discussion another day.

LUKE: Yes, your rough writing—not to mention your actual grammatical errors—might be interesting to discuss another time.

MARK: Let's return to the topic at hand, OK?

LUKE: We should. I had no problem including that story despite my discomfort with the topic and her unusual actions. Apparently, many women have problems related to their . . . ah . . . ability to bear children, and so this story resonates with the common experience of many of them. It honors women where they are—it doesn't force them to act like men to be honorable.

MARK: Well, I suppose you have a point, but that's not why I included it. I included it because the woman clearly violates custom in assertively approaching Jesus. She's an example of Jesus's acceptance of bold women.

LUKE: I suppose that's one way to look at it, but she's also meek and self-effacing: she has no intention of making a scene—of drawing attention from the crowd or from Jesus. She approaches him in a way that many women would find comfortable. Her story shows that Jesus responds well to that kind of approach—he doesn't need women to act like men to merit his attention.

MARK: That's a suspect reading! She might not have approached him loudly, but he himself insisted that she in fact would take center stage and draw the attention of the crowd. His response shows that her supposedly "meek"—although I think you might be misusing that word there—approach wasn't necessary or even appropriate. And while you criticize me for not pairing stories by gender as you did, I did sandwich this story inside that of the raising of Jairus' daughter precisely to show (among other things) that the woman's interaction with Jesus was on par with that of a synagogue leader who, of course, was male.

LUKE: Interesting how you and I tell almost identical stories but understand them so very differently, isn't it?

MARK: I suppose we aren't the first—and we won't be the last—to do that.

LUKE: Indeed. I included your story about Simon's mother-in-law, you know. That is another one which honors women in their usual roles, and I learned about that healing straight from you!

MARK: What? No! She wasn't in a typically female role.

LUKE: Of course she was. She was healed and then served them dinner.

MARK: She didn't just serve them dinner! She served them, yes, but it's no coincidence that when Jesus later describes his ministry, he says that he didn't come to be served but to serve—a line, I might note, which you omitted. I only use that verb for Jesus, angels, and women in order to show that women can—and should!—serve in the same way that not only men but angels and Jesus himself serve.

LUKE: But Mark, how can you miss the nuance that this is stereotypically female service—serving people food—that is the topic here? Yes, Jesus picks up that language, but that's the point: it honors the kinds of things that women traditionally do. Perhaps I should have included that line . . .

MARK: Regardless, one of the points I was trying to make with that healing story is to show women serving as men serve.

LUKE: Well, one of the points I was trying to make with it was to show that the ways in which women traditionally serve are honorable in themselves—women don't have to do what men do in order to be honorable.

MARK: Again I am amazed at how we can interpret the same story so very differently!

LUKE: Me, too.

Amulek and Alma: Atonement

Joseph M. Spencer

I've imagined here a conversation between two scriptural figures who actually interact a good deal in the text: Alma and Amulek. I've done so, however, because I believe there are real tensions, never worked out in the text, between their respective conceptions of the atonement. I've set the conversation in the land of Jershon, immediately after Alma and Amulek have returned from the Zoramite mission, but before the other missionaries have arrived. I've provided footnotes to scriptural passages where they might prove helpful for closer study.

* * * * * * *

AMULEK: Did I hear right about Corianton?[1] I didn't want to believe the gossipers, but I already had my suspicions that something was up. He didn't, did he?

ALMA: He did. I hardly know what to think.

AMULEK: He's a kid—a big dumb ox. . . . Oh, I'm sorry. I don't mean it that way. I just mean he's young, and he isn't thinking. He's spent too many years being praised—good-looking, athletic. It's gone to his head, don't you think?[2]

ALMA: That's got *something* to do with it, anyway.

AMULEK: What? You think there's more?

---

1. See Alma 39:3.
2. See Alma 39:2.

ALMA: You know me. I can't help thinking there's something he doesn't get. About the gospel, I mean.[3] About the very stuff he was supposed to be teaching the Zoramites!

AMULEK: You think he's confused about doctrine, and that that's enough to get him doing something so stupid?

ALMA: Well, I think I'd want to call it theology, not doctrine. But, yeah. I think that's the problem.

AMULEK: Where's he getting screwy ideas about "theology"?

ALMA: How honest do you want me to be?

AMULEK: Why? Who are you going to offend?

ALMA: Well, I . . . Amulek, I'm worried he got the wrong idea from *you*.

AMULEK: You're kidding me. Come on, now. What's really going on?

ALMA: I'm serious. Your teaching in Antionum[4]—there are issues, and I think they might be encouraging my son to . . . Well, you know.

AMULEK: You can't really mean that I'm promoting that sort of behavior!

ALMA: Not exactly. But I wonder if you haven't given Corianton some kind of license to do whatever he wants. . . . Not intentionally, I realize! But nonetheless.

AMULEK: Alright, let's hear it. We've been brothers long enough I think I can take it.

ALMA: I hope you can. So here's the thing. I wonder if you've got the atonement wrong.

AMULEK: The atonement! The heart of the gospel! You don't mean—

---

3. See Alma 39–42.
4. See Alma 34.

ALMA: Yes, the atonement. The way you were talking about it with the Zoramites was unlike anything I've come across, and I've been reading the prophets for a long time.

AMULEK: I thought I was just repeating Abinadi's teachings.[5] How many times have I heard those over the pulpit? How many times have I read that sermon? Sometimes I think it's all I know.

ALMA: I heard you repeating Abinadi's teachings back when we were in Ammonihah seven years ago.[6] Christ "shall take upon him the transgressions of those who believe on his name," but "the wicked remain as though there had been no redemption made, except it be the loosing of the bands of death."[7] That's what I remember you saying back then, and that's pure Abinadi.[8] I said as much when I followed you up in response to Zeezrom![9] But there's something new in your preaching lately. A heavy emphasis on sacrifice, for instance.[10] Where's that coming from?

AMULEK: Sacrifice? Well, I've been reading Father Lehi. You know his father-son chat with Jacob on the fall and the atonement.[11] I've memorized the passage: "The Holy Messiah . . . offereth himself a sacrifice for sin, to answer the ends of the law."[12] I've been trying to make sense of that one line, and I think I've begun to understand it.

ALMA: Yeah, Lehi *does* mention sacrifice. But just that once, and Abinadi never said anything about it. Nor my father. And *I've* never talked that way. No one in the Nephite prophetic tradition talks that way, except for that one line in Lehi's teachings . . . and now you. And anyway, Lehi used it once—in a passage you'll admit is really difficult—but you used it like ten times! You invented a whole theology of sacrifice! And I can't figure out what half of what you said even means: "a great and last sacrifice," "an

---

5. See Mosiah 11–17.
6. See Alma 8–14.
7. Alma 11:40–41.
8. Mosiah 16:5.
9. Alma 12:16–18.
10. See Alma 34:10–16.
11. See 2 Nephi 2.
12. 2 Nephi 2:7.

infinite and eternal sacrifice."[13] What are you getting at? No one I've read talks that way!

AMULEK: I thought I was clear. A human being can't suffer in someone else's place and satisfy justice. No judge would let that happen![14] But God *does* let something like that happen. So Christ's death, which Abinadi made perfectly clear to us—that's got to be something non-human. It isn't finite like the sacrifices we offer. It's got to be infinite. It's got to break every boundary, making sacrifice *work*.[15] Because it doesn't work otherwise. No sacrifice we've ever witnessed can break every boundary. Even the sacrifices we offer under Moses's law seem to me more symbolic than actually effective. I mean I don't think they're *actually* vicarious, just *symbolic* of the one actually vicarious sacrifice still to come.

ALMA: Fine, I suppose, but is that the point? Is that what Lehi means? I don't think so.

AMULEK: Well, okay. I've brought in a bit of Jacob's teachings as well. "It must needs be an infinite atonement."[16] Jacob seems to have understood his father's teachings clearly. Christ offers himself a sacrifice for sin, and it has to be infinite. Otherwise, it can't be vicarious.

ALMA: Hang on. You're cherry-picking. I know Jacob's sermon on the atonement inside and out. He says that the atonement has to be infinite so that the resurrection will happen, not so that the atonement can be vicarious.[17] I can quote the very words: "Save it should be an infinite atonement this corruption could not put on incorruption. Wherefore, the first judgment which came upon man"—he's talking about the "thou shalt surely die" business from the Garden of Eden—"the first judgment which came upon man must needs have remained to an endless duration. And if so, this flesh must have laid down to rot and to crumble to its mother earth, to rise no more."[18] That's perfectly clear, I think. Jacob's trying to tell us that Christ's work has to be infinite if it's to raise rotting flesh from the

---

13. Alma 34:10.

14. See Alma 34:11–12.

15. See Alma 34:13.

16. 2 Nephi 9:7.

17. See 2 Nephi 9:5–16.

18. 2 Nephi 9:7.

grave. It's only you who wants to make the infinite atonement something to fix "the sins of the world," as you put it in Antionum.[19]

AMULEK: Huh. Okay. But I still think Lehi's clear on this. "He offereth himself a sacrifice for sin, to answer the ends of the law."[20] Justice can't be satisfied unless there's a sacrifice. And I think I've put together the mechanism to make sense of that.

ALMA: But Lehi says nothing about justice. Not a word—except to say that a lack of law or opposition would "destroy" it.[21] And notice that he never talks about satisfaction either. It isn't justice that needs satisfying, according to Lehi. It's the law, or rather its ends, that need answering. Whatever's going on with his reference to sacrifice, it's about answering the ends of the law, not satisfying justice.

AMULEK: But what else could the ends of the law be except justice? And what does "answering" mean if it doesn't mean something like satisfaction? You're just getting picky about words now.

ALMA: Hardly. Actually, I think I've been able to put together a clear picture in my head of what Lehi's after, and it informs all my own thinking about these matters.

AMULEK: You think there's a different way to read all this?

ALMA: Yeah. But I don't want to get too distracted by all this right now. Let's talk about Lehi's theology of the atonement later. For the moment, I just wanted to convince you that you haven't got all the details right. But I don't think it's just the heavy emphasis on sacrifice that could make Corianton feel so arrogantly justified in what he's doing. Really, it's the theological assumptions *behind* the way you've been talking about sacrifice that have me worried. I think you called this "the intent" of the sacrifice when you were talking to the Zoramites.[22]

AMULEK: Okay. Go on.

---

19. Alma 34:12.
20. 2 Nephi 2:7.
21. 2 Nephi 2:12.
22. Alma 34:15.

ALMA: Well, here's what I remember you saying: "the intent of this last sacrifice"—Christ's, that is—is "to bring about the bowels of mercy, which overpowereth justice, and bringeth about means unto men that they may have faith unto repentance. And thus mercy can satisfy the demands of justice, and encircles them in the arms of safety."[23]

AMULEK: Right. Otherwise people are "exposed to the whole law of the demands of justice." It's "only unto him that has faith unto repentance" that there's "brought about the great and eternal plan of redemption."[24] That's just Abinadi again. "Therefore he is as though there was no redemption made, being an enemy to God."[25]

ALMA: Well, it *sounds* like Abinadi in a way. But it *isn't* Abinadi. Look, what's this talk about the bowels of mercy overpowering justice? Abinadi never talks that way.

AMULEK: Oh yes, he does! Christ will ascend to heaven, "having the bowels of mercy; being filled with compassion towards the children of men; standing betwixt them and justice; having broken the bands of death, taken upon himself their iniquity and their transgressions, having redeemed them, and satisfied the demands of justice."[26] It's all there, isn't it? And whatever *you* can't find in Lehi (but *I* can) is right there in Abinadi too: the satisfaction of justice's demands by vicarious punishment, in addition to the bowels of mercy getting human beings out of justice's grasp.

ALMA: Okay, okay. Let's take this more slowly, shall we? Whatever *Abinadi* says, I hear *you* making two foundational claims. First, that it's "faith unto repentance" that brings salvation.[27] Is that right?

AMULEK: Certainly.

ALMA: Second, then, that what makes for "faith unto repentance" is the way that "mercy . . . overpowereth justice."[28] Yes?

---

23. Alma 34:15–16.
24. Alma 34:16.
25. Mosiah 16:5.
26. Mosiah 15:9.
27. Alma 34:15.
28. Alma 34:15.

AMULEK: Right. I mean something like this: when we as human beings see that God condescends to take up flesh, and that he's so submissive to the will of the Spirit that he becomes a sacrifice for our sins, we begin to believe that it's possible to be forgiven. Faith that leads to repentance becomes a real possibility. We can't muster the will to change if we don't first see that Christ's sacrifice makes change possible.

ALMA: Okay. Let's say I buy all that, though I'm still nervous about your references to sacrifice. Let's say I buy the idea that we can't muster the will to change until we trust the angelic word, which announces that God himself has made change possible. That's fine. But then you go on to assume something about the way God makes change possible. You say it's a matter of mercy overpowering justice.

AMULEK: Yeah, like Abinadi said: Christ "stands betwixt us and justice" because he "has the bowels of mercy."[29]

ALMA: You don't think there's a difference between "standing betwixt something and justice" and "overpowering justice"?[30] You talk as if Christ will have wrestled justice into submission. I don't hear that in Abinadi's words.

AMULEK: Well, we have to be shielded from justice, at any rate!

ALMA: Maybe. Is that so clear? Justice has to be put at a distance from us, at least for a time. It's not clear to me that we're not to come directly into relation to it later on. See, the problem, I think, is that you want to separate justice from God, treating it as if it were some kind of cosmic force, an isolable and independent thing. You speak only abstractly of justice,[31] but I speak always of the justice of God.[32] Justice isn't something over against God. It's a feature or an aspect or an attribute of God himself. Let me put this sharply, since I think I'm going to have to put it to Corianton this way: *If it weren't for the right conditions, mercy could only operate by destroying the work of God's justice. But the work of justice can't be destroyed. If it were, God would cease to be God.*[33]

---

29. Mosiah 15:9.
30. Mosiah 15:9; Alma 34:15.
31. Alma 34:15–16.
32. Alma 41:2, 3; 42:1, 14, 30.
33. Alma 42:13.

AMULEK: Whoa. Slow down. God would cease to be God? Aren't you bordering on blasphemy there? I was once accused of speaking as if I had authority to command God.[34] I almost wonder if you shouldn't be accused of that now!

ALMA: Nonsense. I'm doing exactly what you were rightly doing when you were accused of the same thing.[35] I can't deny God's word on this point, and in God's word I find him associating himself so closely with justice that to separate God and justice would be to make God not-God.

AMULEK: I can't get comfortable with that way of talking, but let's ignore that for the moment. You want to make justice immanent to God. That's a good "theological" way of putting it, no?

ALMA: That's right. And I want to say that God's justice has a proper *work* to do, something that's bound up with God's very being.[36]

AMULEK: What's that?

ALMA: Let's call it "restoration."[37] That's a good Abinadite word.[38] And it's one you used, if I remember right, back when we were teaching in Ammonihah.[39]

AMULEK: Sure. Say more, then. I'm assuming we'll soon get to what any of this has to do with Corianton?

ALMA: I'm getting there. Abinadi and you have used the word to talk about the effect of the resurrection. You said something like this: "Every thing shall be restored to its perfect frame, as it is now, or in the body."[40] Let's call this *special* restoration. But I'm interested also in what might be called *general* restoration—what I think I'd like to call "the plan of restoration."[41] Here I've got in mind a much wider phenomenon, the idea

---

34. Alma 11:34–35.
35. Alma 11:36–37.
36. Alma 42:13.
37. Alma 41:1.
38. Mosiah 15:24.
39. Alma 11:44.
40. Alma 11:44.
41. Alma 41:2.

that all things should be restored to their proper order. That, I think, is, shall we say, *requisite* with the justice of God. "Requisite": I'm choosing that word carefully. It's absolutely necessary, given God's inalienable justice, that everything eventually be brought back to its proper order. Things must become what they are.[42]

AMULEK: Okay. That's going more than a bit beyond Abinadi's use of the word "restoration," though.

ALMA: Fair enough. But it's not unconnected with what Abinadi has to say. I think *special* restoration (resurrection) is what makes *general* restoration (all things coming back to their proper order) possible. We can't fulfill the *plan* of restoration without there being first the raising of mortality to immortality, corruption to incorruption—that is, without Abinadi's sort of restoration. The one conditions the other.[43]

AMULEK: Aren't these two different senses of "restoration"? In the one case, the emphasis is on *bringing* something *back*, but in the other, it's on *what's* brought back.

ALMA: Sure, I'm fine with that. Maybe better: special restoration does the *bringing* of bringing back, while general restoration focuses on the *back* of bringing back. But these are just cute slogans. What's really important is that all this is tied to God's justice. The resurrection isn't directly required by God's justice, but the restoration of all things to their proper order sure is. And that isn't possible without the resurrection. So both end up being required by God's justice.[44]

AMULEK: I've got the picture, I think. Now give me the "So what?"

ALMA: Well, here's the thing. It's only when we put this whole picture together that we can see that mercy can't *rob* justice, like you seem to claim.[45] Rather, mercy just *postpones* justice for a time. Everything will be brought back to its proper order, but we've got a little bit of a breathing space in which we can change things. God didn't execute Adam and Eve the second

---

42. See Alma 41:2, 5–6.
43. Alma 41:3–4.
44. Alma 41:2–3.
45. Alma 42:25.

they ate the fruit, right?[46] And he's given us a probationary state as well.[47] If our natures change during that time, then we'll eventually be restored to what'll have become our proper nature.[48]

AMULEK: I don't disagree with any of this. I've been calling people to repentance at your side for a long time, Alma.

ALMA: I know. But you've recently been making justice into the irreparable bad guy when you've been preaching with me—at least among the Zoramites. You've been preaching for years with Zeezrom in Melek before we asked you to join us in Antionum.[49] I assume you've been making justice the irreparable bad guy there too?

AMULEK: Let's not assume too much.

ALMA: Fine. But look, justice *isn't* the bad guy, as your metaphors suggest. It's the good guy—part of God in fact! I see, of course, that it *can become* the bad guy if there's no plan of mercy, no postponement of its effects for a time. Then it's the bad guy because we can't change into what we'd like to see brought back in the fulfilled plan of general restoration.[50] But you seem to want it to be the bad guy right now (and always). And so you think punishment has to be meted out for all we've already done wrong, and our repentance redirects that punishment to Christ. *I'd* say rather that we've got to change through repentance so that *when* justice finally *does* have full sway, it's to our benefit, rather than to our everlasting shame. There'll be punishment, sure, but only for those who haven't repented.[51] And those who escape punishment don't do so because Christ suffered that punishment in our place, as if some abstract cosmic justice had to be balanced by someone's infinite suffering. Rather, we escape because he's inspired us to change, and he can restore us to what we've become.

AMULEK: So you don't think justice makes any demands? There's nothing to be satisfied?

---

46. Alma 42:2–4.
47. Alma 42:8–10.
48. Alma 41:13–15.
49. Alma 31:6.
50. Alma 42:14.
51. Alma 42:22.

ALMA: Sure, justice makes demands.[52] And those demands will have to be satisfied. But I think the demands will be satisfied only *eventually*, when all's said and done. And I think the only relevant demands it makes concern the restoration of all things to their proper order.[53] I don't see it making any demands regarding some kind of cosmic fairness, some balance of punishment and reward.

AMULEK: Have I disagreed with any of this?

ALMA: I think so. You replace the plan of restoration—justice radically fulfilled—with the plan of non-restoration—justice robbed by mercy.[54]

AMULEK: Hang on. You used that language a minute ago, and you're using it again now. I've never said that mercy robs justice.

ALMA: Isn't something like that what you mean when you talk of overpowering?[55]

AMULEK: I don't think so. I can picture all kinds of situations where you might overpower someone without robbing them!

ALMA: But you don't rob a house without binding the strong man, do you?[56] You have to overpower in order to rob. The one leads to the other. You overpower *so* that you can rob.

AMULEK: But you don't have to rob anything. Can't you overpower an enemy simply because he's dangerous, without any intention to rob him?

ALMA: Yeah, okay. But you talk as if justice had us in its grasp, and we've got to be rescued. Don't you mean that mercy overpowers justice so that it can steal us back?

---

52. Alma 42:15, 24.
53. Alma 41:2.
54. Alma 42:25.
55. Alma 34:15.
56. See Mark 3:27.

AMULEK: Wouldn't *you* want to say that justice grasps, and that we want out of that grasp?[57]

ALMA: Well, yes. But I don't want to say that we should get *entirely* out of that grasp. We just want to get out of the grasp of its *premature* application, which would cut off the possibility of any redemption.

AMULEK: So you too want mercy to rob justice! You just plan to have mercy return what's been stolen once it's changed in nature—or failed to change, as the case may be. But you still want justice to be robbed, don't you? You still want it overpowered, if only for a time. Mercy still has to "stand betwixt" human beings and justice.[58]

ALMA: Right, but now we've come back to the two ways to read that metaphor. Does Christ with the bowels of mercy stand between us and justice because justice has been vanquished? Or does he stand between us and justice because he's put justice at a temporary distance from us?

AMULEK: Okay, I'll concede there's a difference there. But what's the difference worth? Is there any practical upshot? I guess I'm asking what all this has to do, at last, with Corianton. Let's say there's a real difference at the theoretical level between our ways of talking about what's behind the atonement. How could what I've been teaching lead Corianton—or anyone!—to sin? I've been calling for repentance as strenuously as you have. And I think I can see ways in which my conception calls all the more urgently for repentance than does your model.

ALMA: Well, if justice ends up overpowered, permanently put out of play, then God can only look *unjust* if he condemns anyone to punishment. That's the way I think Corianton's thinking about things.[59] And you see perfectly well where *that's* led him. If God's unjust simply for punishing sinners, then why should he feel guilty if he does anything wrong? If God punishes him for his arrogant sins, it's *God* who should feel guilty! Isn't that what Corianton's thinking?

---

57. Alma 42:14.
58. Mosiah 15:9.
59. Alma 42:1.

AMULEK: But that'd be true only if Abinadi were wrong. I mean, God could be thought unjust for punishing the wicked only if the wicked didn't remain as though there were no redemption.[60]

ALMA: So you want justice to scare people into repentance because only then mercy can take effect?

AMULEK: Isn't that what you want too?

ALMA: Well, sort of. Yeah, I guess.[61] Or rather, I want justice *without mercy* to scare people into repentance because only then can justice *with mercy* take effect.

AMULEK: So there's little difference between what we're saying, right? It's just that you want to make sure that justice secures the restoration of all things to their proper order, and so you want to make sure that mercy doesn't discombobulate it. But we both want people to find mercy so that justice isn't a terror. Or perhaps we both want people to see the terror of merciless justice so that they'll seek mercy.

ALMA: Yeah, that seems right.

AMULEK: So maybe Corianton's taken advantage in some way of my theology, but I haven't given him license to sin. Right?

ALMA: Okay, I think you're right. Maybe we're just rival theologians after all: speculators who get thinking because we have practical questions, and who start to think we've got deep points of disagreement about practical matters—but who find, in the end, that we've got more or less the same practical solutions, even if we've constructed contrasting systems.

AMULEK: Theologians, yes.

ALMA: Theologians who apologize for thinking ill of one another?

AMULEK: I hope so.

---

60. See Mosiah 16:5.
61. Alma 42:30.

ALMA: Well, I hope you know my good will. I've got some further thinking to do in the meanwhile, since I've got to talk to Corianton about all this as soon as he's here.[62] After this, I'm not entirely sure what I want to say to him. I'll certainly be leaving your name out of it.

AMULEK: Well, and I've got to leave for Melek again. There's a lot to get ready if you think we'll want to move the Ammonites over there for safety's sake.[63] Let's hope it doesn't come to that, though. You'll come see me soon, won't you? I'd love to sit down with Lehi's sermon and see what you've got to say about it.

ALMA: Yeah, I'll make my way there once some things are settled.[64] I'd like to retire out there, joining you and Zeezrom. So as soon as things are in order here—and in Zarahemla (oh, that's a headache!)[65]—I'll come to see you in Melek.

AMULEK: Beautiful. But don't come alone. The road between Zarahemla and Melek isn't terribly safe these days. Who knows what could happen to you on the way?

ALMA: Who knows? Who knows, indeed![66]

---

62. See Alma 39–42.
63. See Alma 35:13–14.
64. See Alma 45:18.
65. See Alma 35:15–16 and Alma 45–49.
66. See Alma 45:18–19.

Balaam and Daniel: Prophecy

Walter E. A. van Beek

BALAAM: Greetings, my ancient friend and colleague, greetings from the borders of Palestine. Give my regards to your Median king, the one you serve at the moment—there were so many in your long and highly successful career as king's counselor, I lost track.[1] For several reasons I will try to use this wonderful new invention of e-mail, where one sends a message quicker than a galloping horse and can expect an answer faster than the flight of the falcon. I need that speed for I am in trouble. It is a long time since we first met, and we have been out of contact for ages, or so it seems, but I dare to address you now in order to solicit your help in a time of distress. Please, help me, for my enemies have laid a siege on me, my detractors are weaving a web of lies around me, and I fear for my life. During your life at the Persian—now Median—court, you must have become an expert in surviving court intrigues, and I sorely need your expert advice. Remember when the four of you were ordered to eat the meat at the king's table, and drink his wine; all of you refused and made a wager with your

---

1. Daniel is quite the ideal legendary figure in the biblical account. The Book of Daniel was written in its present form between 167 and 164 B.C.E. It can be pinpointed accurately due to the last chapters, which describe the wars of the most hated king in the history of Israel, Antiochus IV, called Epiphanes, a Seleucid king (the succession line of Alexander the Great) who tried to destroy Jewish worship in the temple at that time. But the name of Daniel as an exemplary example of righteousness, together with Noah and Job, is mentioned already by Ezekiel. These three form the heroes of this prophet of the Babylonian exile (Ezek. 14:14); all three of them are legendary and belong to a Babylonian mythic past. Their stories have been filled in by Hebrew scribes much later and imbued with an Israelite theology. The fictional nature of the figure of Daniel in no way detracts from the message of his stories; neither does the non-fictional character of the other figure, Balaam, adds to the credibility of his story. This is about stories, not about histories. In this dialogue both stories are taken as they go, without any consideration of historicity.

overseer that you would come out shining after ten days on a vegetarian diet.[2] The poor man must have feared for his life, responsible as he was for these magnificent foreign hostages of the king, and surely was quite relieved at the end. (I wonder if you turned him into a vegetarian himself?) But pleasantries aside, I am in trouble, could you please support my case?

DANIEL: Quite an unexpected surprise to hear from you, dear son of the venerable Beor,[3] and yes this new invention will facilitate my assistance. Of course I am willing to help you; I have had my share of trouble here at the court. Jealousy raised its ugly green head many times, but things seem to be calmer now with the Medes having replaced the Persians. What exactly do you want from me? Not all wisdom is under my command—you should not believe the praise singers at the court—but dear old Babylon holds a tremendous store of experience and a host of wise men, among whom I have some influence. So, what is your problem?

BALAAM: Thanks, dear friend and esteemed colleague, I knew I could count on you. The problem is simple: people accuse me of being a false prophet, first, and of ruining the Israelite nation, second. The grapevine has it that they plan an all-out attack on our city with the explicit aim to kill me. The issue has, as always, a long and complicated history. I have been made a laughing stock by my colleagues, as a wishy-washy prophet, not a serious one. Without any doubt, you have heard rumors of the story with the ass. That is when it started. Israel came into Moab, and the petty kings of the area were scared to death. Balak heard that his old enemies Og and Shihon had been beaten by the invaders, and he sent word to Midian to take joint measures. Evidently, they came to me; they knew I was a prophet of a host of gods, like Ashtarte and Shgr, as well as the Shaddai

---

2. Daniel 1:16–17.

3. Viewing all the improbabilities and even impossibilities of the Balaam story, the most astonishing fact is that Balaam actually existed. At Deir Alla, in the Jordan River Valley, just at the Palestinian side, a team of Dutch archaeologists have found a major inscription on a wall, citing prophecies of a certain *BLM bn BR*, which I will refer to later in the discussion. He seems to have been an important prophetic figure in the area, so the notion that he was involved as a religious authority in the defense of the inhabitants against invading Israel is plausible.

gods,[4] so they reckoned I had a line with the Hebrew god as well.[5] Trusting in my calling, they asked me to curse the newcomers, those Hebrew tribes who covered the Moab plain like locusts. Even if they just had lost their revered leader, an Egyptian guy, that seemed not to deter them. To my own surprise, that very night the Hebrew god—they refrain from giving him a proper name, insisting that he simply is what he is, so just call him the Lord—did speak to me and forbade me to curse Israel, as he had a special aim with them. So I sent word to Balak, that the answer was no.[6]

DANIEL: That seems pretty straightforward: Yahweh—that is the name we use, or Elohim—chose you as one of his prophets, and you did as he bade. And you being a gentile at that, quite an honor to be the Lord's mouthpiece. But what was that story with the ass? You know I have a special relationship with animals. When my enemies at court sought my downfall, they did so cleverly. They tricked the king into an edict that no-body should for one month venerate any god but the king. That was silly, for the king of Persia, Darius, was follower of Zoroaster and would never set himself up as a god, but they somehow got his signature on a decree, and once issued, an edict cannot be revoked. Of course, I just prayed to Yahweh as usual, and there they had me. Darius was furious at them, but had to follow his own document. He personally came to see me descend into the lions' den, the good man. That was a night to remember, I have to tell you, but the beasts were very friendly and let me go unharmed.

---

4. These gods are mentioned in the text in Deir Alla. Not all of these are completely clear.

5. In the early parts of the Old Testament, the God of Israel posits himself as the only god *for* Israel, not for all of the world. The presence of other gods is acknowledged, though resented. The commandment in the Decalogue not to bow before other gods cannot be read as a denial of their existence but as being in competition with them. It is only after the Babylonian Exile that Yahweh or Elohim—they often are used interchangeably, depending on the origin of the grounding text—is truly recognized as a monotheistic god, where other gods become non-existent.

6. Numbers 22–24 gives this story with astonishing detail, especially considering the fact that there were no Hebrews present at the events. The story reads as a pastiche, a satire on a prophet or prophethood as experienced at the time of the editing of the Old Testament (i.e., after the Babylonian Exile). As such it belongs to the same genre as Jonah and the Fish, and may have served well the political and religious factions that were pitted against each other at the time of the first return from Babylon.

Animals are wonderful, real instruments of the Lord, and much misrepresented. Was your ass of the same persuasion?

BALAAM: Yes, I think so, at least it appeared to be much more than the simple mount I thought it was. Anyway, from Balak came a delegation of high priests with a nice bundle of money, insisting I do my work. Well worth a reconsideration. OK, so that night I asked the Lord again whether he would permit me to go, viewing the circumstances. And he acquiesced, providing I would say the words that he would put in my mouth. Well, that is my usual procedure anyway, that is why we are called prophets after all, isn't it?

DANIEL: Yes, actually in my own cases of prophecy I never knew what to say to my king before I actually stood before him. He even demanded knowledge he knew I could not have, like explanation of dreams, mind you not my dreams, but his own. He used to test me against my competitors, those Zoroastrian sages, realizing it could only be the Lord that gave me the information. Yes, speaking what the Lord tells you to speak is the gist of our calling, and the Lord never ceases to surprise.

BALAAM: You can say that again. For when I set out in the morning he suddenly seemed very angry and sent an angel to block my way. At first I did not see the angel, who was invisible as far as I was concerned, but my donkey saw him all right. I spurred it on, and then it started to speak, reminding me of her faithful services: Why was I forcing her against her will? Then I saw the angel myself, and he told me that he had spared my life because of the donkey. I apologized for my reaction, also to the donkey, and was allowed to go on. It still puzzles me why the Lord changed his mind and set out to kill me after agreeing with my journey. Any idea?

DANIEL: If the Lord changes his mind he probably has a good reason for it, but it is not always clear what that is. That Israel leader, Moses was his name, had the same experience several times: once the Lord suddenly wanted to kill him, but desisted at the pleas of his wife.[7] This incident remains a mystery, actually. At some other time he even wanted to kill off the whole of Israel because they were headstrong and stubborn. Then Moses stepped in and argued that the Lord would look pretty ludicrous saving a people first with mighty deeds, only to destroy them later. And

---

7. Exodus 24:4.

the Lord listened to him.[8] We as his colleagues just surmise that the Lord tested Moses whether he stood his ground as a leader pleading for his tribe. Maybe he was testing you as well, whether you would keep the plan; or, maybe to see how you treated animals, who knows? But as a prophet you are much more than a simple mouthpiece—you are expected to use your own good judgment as well. We have agency, you know, also vis à vis the Lord.

BALAAM: That is a relief, and I will use this against my accusers. For some say I should not have tried to persuade the Lord at all, but obey blindly, without debate. I think they simply do not like the idea of a prophet of the Lord who is not part of Israel. Anyway, such blind obedience is beneath our stature, beneath anyone's. Well, the assignment went pretty well. Balak took me to a hillside—Kirjat-Husot, you would not know the place if you have never been back to Palestine—made sacrifices on seven altars, and then looked at me. I spoke up, but out of my mouth came a series of blessings of Israel. Balak was furious and thought I had the wrong impression of the invaders, so he took me to Bamot-Baal—you may have heard of this mountain, pretty high, just look it up with Google Earth—to have a better look. My word, there were a lot of them, the whole plain was covered with these people, but the same was repeated: large sacrifices and out came a blessing, an even better one; and that at a Baal shrine! After the third failed attempt at cursing, at Mount Pisgah, Balak became very angry. Actually I feared for my life, but my response to his threats was a prophecy on him and his mates, even on some people I have never heard of. Kittim, you have heard of them?

DANIEL: At least I know one of these mountains, Pisgah was the one where Moses had his one and only look at the promised land, so you were on historical ground.[9] And, yes, Kittim seems to be a powerful empire that will come at the end of times. In one of my prophecies they figure with their ships.[10] They come from overseas, a place they call Rome over there.[11] But why did not Balak kill you? You took his money and did not

---

8. Numbers 14.

9. Deuteronomy 34:1–4.

10. Daniel 11:30.

11. Numbers 24:23–24. Kittim is the name the Roman empire is referred to in the Dead Sea Scrolls. In the Qumran community, the Book of Daniel was extremely popular—even if it had been written just a few decades earlier—and this was their

do what he had asked. Both my Persian and Median kings would have had no compunction; I had to be saved by stronger means than just the words of God. I needed miracles; once I even had to emerge unscathed from a fiery pit.

BALAAM: Yeah, I heard about that one; it has become quite famous in the region. In my case, I think Balak may have been impressed by my manner of prophesying; bystanders later told me that I was completely in a trance, and he was scared, and so were the others. Whatever their political aims were, those kings recognized the word of prophecy. Actually, I learned from the bystanders what exactly I had said, because I seem to recall very little of it myself. Good that people write these words down. Isn't Aramaic a wonderful language for prophecy!

DANIEL: Yes, the same holds for me; I did not write myself either, but both in Aramaic and Hebrew the words of God came down on parchment through great scribes.[12] Whoever wields the writing stick will in the end rule the world—mark my words. So far, so good; all I can say is that you did well, putting up with self-centered rulers and a rather fickle Lord. You even apologized to your ass; what more can one ask? If that is all the case they have, your enemies should be thrown out of court. Mine fared quite badly; most of them were killed off by the king, and in these days nobody dares to point a finger at me any longer.

BALAAM: Well, the main issue comes now; being ridiculed hurts less than the prospect of being killed. When I later met Balak, he asked me why I had not heeded the contract. "It was the Lord who spoke," I told him, "but if you want to harm Israel, you have to use other means." Then I explained to him that the Israelite God, whom I knew better now, was quite peculiar with food, with sex, and with what they call idols, meaning the other gods. Those Israelites live under a tight regime, and he is known to be extremely displeased when they misbehave. And when he is displeased, you better take cover, also his own people. That was new to Balak, and is still strange to me; usually our gods are pleased when you do

---

dominant interpretation. In many apocalyptic texts of the second and first century, the Roman empire embodies the principle of evil, like in John's apocalypse.

12. Aramaic was the lingua franca of the region at the time of writing the Book of Daniel, just as it was the language that Jesus used. The Book of Daniel is partly in Hebrew, partly in Aramaic.

the rituals correctly, speak the truth and avoid wrong doings, like stealing or murder. That should be enough, I think. What do your Persians think?

DANIEL: I told you Zoroastrianism is the cult of the realm,[13] and they are quite moral, one has to say. Indeed, the proper rituals, honesty, respect for parents and elders, no lying, no stealing, not killing anyone else but your enemies; their motto is speak straight and shoot straight. I never had problems in this sphere, but the point is that for us Israelites the relationship does not stop there: we have a much more personal link to the Lord, expressed as covenant, a kind of personal contract. Some seemingly trivial conditions are stipulated, a lot of them having to do with food. That is why me and my friends refused to eat from the king's table, and that is why we will not eat meat from other sacrifices than to Yahweh. This abstinence is not unhealthy, like my bout of vegetarianism did me good, but the rules are mainly a marker, a way to define oneself as belonging to the Lord, his covenant people. We have to keep apart. Marrying strangers is one of these rules, less trivial, even quite crucial. One has to avow however that our leaders often did marry foreign women, me included. I followed there the example of Moses, Joseph, Boaz, even the great-grandmother of none other than our supreme king, David. The point seems to be not so much the women themselves, but the worship of other gods. That is the real issue, it appears.

BALAAM: That explains a lot of the reactions we found puzzling. Balak followed my advice and for him it worked out well. He sent women to Israel, the maidens of his realm and, of course, some experienced ladies from the Baal temples. Quite harmless, he thought, this could never be a weapon; if the Israelites knew the ways of the world, they simply would have fun and move on. I knew by then that this was not so simple, and I expected them to reject the ladies. In fact I saw this as a test case, a little bit like your abstention from wine. I heard the Lord had often used other people as tests for the fidelity of Israel, hasn't he?

---

13. Darius indeed made Zoroastrianism into the official religion of his empire; this religion has been a major inspiration also for the Jews in exile, and many traces of this religion that is reportedly the oldest religion with a written script in the world, are discernible in the Old Testament. One of these is the notion of the End of Times, a theme that permeates the genre of apocalypse, to which the Book of Daniel belongs.

DANIEL: Yes, quite often, in fact. Starting out in Egypt, then through-out the years of desert wandering, and right through my time, the Lord has almost routinely used other people to harass Israel after transgression, and to more or less force them back to his law and their joint covenant. Quite a list they make: Amalikites, Edomites Moabites, and especially the Philistines. Even within Israel he tested their faithfulness between the two halves of their realm, North and South, the descendants of Joseph and of Judah. So, indeed, you did what he often does and probably will keep doing. There is one catch though: you are not God, and even if you are his prophet, that test could only be put to Israel on his command, not your own initiative.

BALAAM: Ay, there is the rub! There is the respect that makes calamity of so short a life.[14] Maybe I should have asked the Lord first. Anyway, Israel fell for it lock, stock and barrel; I never witnessed anything like it. The Israelite men reacted as any true-blooded man would: they went for the ladies and to humor them sacrificed to Baal. But on the other hand the lush ladies of the lands of milk and honey might have been too much to resist for men who had wandered in the desert for forty years, with their women just as desert-hardened as they themselves.

DANIEL: Well, the Lord is not against marriage, even if he has said very little about it through his prophets, but the question is again that the Israelites have to keep to themselves. And in this he goes to great length, and can be quite severe. I understand that was the case here as well.

BALAAM: Yes he was, my word, he really was. The Israelite god sent in an epidemic which killed off thousands of them. Some say 24,000, but one can never trust these scribes with numbers; they always add at least one zero.[15] But Balak was thrilled; I was completely reinstated in his grace. His comment was that he did not want their god as an enemy, but surely not as a friend. I am not so sure: despite this terrible punishment, Balak never succeeded in subduing Israel; they still are too strong for him, so he still seems to have Yahweh as a more-than-formidable opponent. Well, this time I kept my mouth shut. I was quite unhappy with this outcome.

---

14. With some apologies to the Great Bard of Stratford-upon-Avon.

15. Numbers in the Old Testament generally have to be interpreted more as either political statements, or as symbolical figures; 24,000 clearly is symbolic: all tribes had been affected, equally and severely.

This was never my intention; at first I was quite impressed with Israel, but they disappointed me, and the Lord's reaction is frightening. But now his bondspeople show themselves an unforgiving enemy. Through our spies I heard that they blamed Balak's stratagem on me, and are now plotting against me, so I am scared, as scared of them as they should be of their God. I would rather be in his grace than in Balak's.

DANIEL: The word of the Lord is not always welcome. You have to account for human frailty, actually a lot, and the Israelite people have disappointed us, as leaders, prophets or scribes, so often we no longer are surprised. Of course everyone seeks a scapegoat, someone to blame for one's mistakes, that is all too human. Actually, they even have the notion of the scapegoat in their law. Each year their high priest has to lay his hands on the head of a black goat, load all the sins of the people onto the poor animal, and then send the goat into the wilderness to perish. Azazel they call that goat, the one that gets away, but it may also mean the demon.[16]

BALAAM: We seem to be back at the animals again. Let me stay with my donkey, at least that is a sacred animal. I fear that the Hebrews are setting me up as the fall guy, what you call a scapegoat while they themselves were the ones that jumped into the arms of our women. They are too strong for us, these Hebrew tribes, and even Balak's favor will not shield me; in fact it condemns me in their eyes. And yet, I remade them from an invading rabble into a blessed presence in this land. You know, when the Lord has blessed a people, that is not simply for this moment, but they are blessed forever; the blessing becomes part of their identity: they are those who are blessed.

DANIEL: I know, and the reverse holds as well. My king, Nebuchadnezzar, has experienced as much; he almost turned into an animal himself after a curse, while Belshazzar was scared to death by the handwriting on the wall. But a real king knows his god, and his god knows him.

BALAAM: Well, I know about writings on a wall, it is one of my lasting legacies.[17] But I know for sure just one thing: the Lord did this through me, I may not be a prophet *from* Israel, but I definitely am a prophet *for*

16. Azazel means "for the entire removal," but the Book of Enoch mentions the name as that of a demon. The equation of Jesus with the scapegoat is common, albeit not dominant—the sacrificial Lamb is more usual.

17. In Deir Alla, at least.

Israel. I spoke with Yahweh, he spoke to me, and I spoke his words to his people, in front of their enemies, while both the Israelites and their enemies acknowledged me as a prophet. My friend, your visions and dreams still are the topic of intense debates. I gather you are aware of that.

DANIEL: Surely I am, and I myself wrestle continuously with them. The dreams themselves were crystal clear, sharp images and frightening events; every time I woke up covered in sweat. Usually I forget my dreams, like almost everyone, but these stayed with me in great detail; in fact I tried to forget them, but they haunted me till I had a scribe record them.

BALAAM: The dream about the statue really got around, but you told me that was not yours. How did this go precisely?

DANIEL: No, it was the king's dream. He was scared to death, but dared not to show it as a king, just summoned his advisers. He was even too scared to tell them the dream, as it might reflect badly on himself and a king is very vulnerable in this sphere; he has to appear strong and daring. So they had to tell him his own dream and what it meant. Nobody could, and our future suddenly became very bleak. The Lord intervened with me, showed me the dream, and explained it. Well, you know, it was about kingdoms to follow our king's one. He was very relieved, and we as advisers could stay alive. But I think my own dreams were much more frightening. They were about animals.

BALAAM: There we are again, with animals. You had friendly lions, I had a wise donkey, so why were these other animals frightening?

DANIEL: I never saw the like. Maybe there are creatures like that at the edge of the world—monstrous beasts—I had a hard time describing them: horns everywhere, wings where there should not be wings, horrible heads, all from the sea.

BALAAM: One never knows what is in the deep of the seas; our colleague Jonah once told me his harrowing experience; that seemed to have been a fish, but he could not identify it—at least not from the inside.

DANIEL: Those beasts in my dream at least kept their distance, I just saw them and hoped they would not see me. In a later dream a ram and a goat featured, but even these were crazy, especially their horns; it was a dream with horns all over the place, and most horns were pure evil.

BALAAM: Any idea what it all meant?

DANIEL: Yes, in fact, an angel explained them to me. They had the same message as the statue: a series of kingdoms ending with the Greek who are called Macedonians. Their inheritors would make war internally, but then the Lord would intervene.[18]

BALAAM: Animals with messages—our lives seem to be punctuated by them. Returning to my present predicament, I do hope the Lord will intervene on my behalf as well, as he did in your case with the king. I would hate to be like the little animal upon which all the sins of Israel are loaded, but I already can imagine how the little beast must have felt. I may have made a mistake, but that is what makes us human. You, on the other hand, seem to come out absolutely perfect in the account of your biographers. My detractors even spread the word that I am extremely ugly, and that is not true. Evidently, I never had your shining countenance, but there are more prophets of the Lord without any visual appeal; remember Eli, remember Jeremiah? Nothing about me can pass muster with my enemies. On the other hand, you seem to have all the goodies in life.

DANIEL: My scribes have been sweet on me; they felt Israel needed a good example at a time when they were in exile and so they really whitewashed my life. Actually, I made my share of mistakes, and surely had my share of enemies at court. Despite the hagiography my scribes turned my life into, they left in one glaring mistake I made, at the end of the book. There I predicted how the evil king would meet his end, and I was completely wrong. I am happy they missed that one; it keeps me human.[19]

---

18. There is no end to the interpretations of Daniel's dreams. Scholarly consensus has it that the book addresses the situation around 164 B.C.E. Any interpretation which carries the predictions into our days has to be considered a creative reinvention of the prophecies. However sympathetic many of these constructed messages might be, they bear little relationship to the actual text and author—who is not Daniel, of course.

19. It is the mistake that allows us to date the book so precisely.

BALAAM: That is gratifying to hear, my dear friend and great example. We speak the words of the Lord, but we still are human. Even as prophets, we are not infallible, nor are the words that come through our mouth. Well, fortune seems to dictate that my mistakes have been served out widely, used against me, and made me also into an example for Israel, but then an example what a prophet should not do. It is not fair!

DANIEL: Life is not always fair at all. Indeed, a people needs its heroes, but also its villains, examples of both kinds. I was lucky to have an extremely good press, almost inhumanly so, and you seem to be on the receiving end of blame. Please derive some comfort from the thought that whatever they will do in the future to your reputation, the fact that you blessed Israel not by your own force, but by the words of the Lord, will stand untarnished by the hands of time. Through you Israel has become a blessed nation, even if you as a gentile were about the last one they expected it from. Nobody can take that away from you.

BALAAM:

DANIEL: Balaam, I got no response to my words of comfort.

BALAAM:

DANIEL: Balaam, Balaam, where are you? Balaam, where art thou? Answer me, my dear friend.

BALAAM:

DANIEL (*somewhat later on his personal website*):

Epitaph for a great prophet

It is with great sadness that I have to announce the death of a great prophet, called Balaam ben Beor. During his last days we have become quite intimate through the web, as he confided his problems to me. He was the prophet that blessed Israel, a gentile prophet that shone at a time when the Israelite prophets were silent. He was the prophet that stood up against his own kings, risking his very life. A humble prophet he was—who could take counsel from his donkey. He had the misfortune of standing between his loyalty to his own people, and to Israel, and he had the deep misfortune that there was no place for both. Of course, as any one of us, the author included, he made his mistakes, in his case his mistake was the test he put Israel to. To me, in our e-mail exchange, he admitted as much, viewing that he had prorogated a task that should have been delegated to him from the Lord, and he hoped he would be forgiven for that. I do think he will, for he was a great prophet, honored by all peoples in the area, speaking with the world of the High Ones with great ease on behalf of whomever came to him with questions and problems. He warned the world where and when he should, he comforted when he could.

He did not deserve this end. Word has it that he was killed brutally, even that he was killed fourfold: stoned, burned, decapitated and strangled. These are extreme measures: Israel really made him into their scapegoat, their Azazel, not even allowing him the gentle desert death allotted to that particular sacrificial victim. Well, if that helps Israel to stay on the straight and narrow, so be it. I know that in the future people will keep referring to his name as a false teacher,[20] and that later prophets will even compare him to a dog.[21] He may have been the prophet-of-the-donkey, but this legacy is unfair. On the other hand, some will compare his demise with another sacrificial victim, another victim of an unjust conviction to come much later, a sacrifice to end all sacrifices,[22] and that does give some comfort. Thus Balaam the prophet, the son of Beor, will be likened to both the worst enemy of the Lord and the great promise of the Lord. For someone who really lived, for any human being who really walked on the face of this earth, what more could be said: he was an example for us all, both in his strength and in his weakness. May his memory never fade.

---

20. See Jude 1:11, 2 Peter 2:15, and Revelation 2:14.

21. Mohammed: Qur'an sura 7, ayat 175–76.

22. Balaam is sometimes compared with Jesus (Sanhedrin 106b, Gitting 57a) or even as a pseudonym for Jesus.

Solomon and Josiah: Writing History

Walter E. A. van Beek

JOSIAH: My most revered and esteemed ancestor, from the far future I have the honor to address you, you who lived in my deep past. Please allow me to introduce myself: I am Josiah son of Amon, king of Judah, and your many-times-great grandson in straight patrilineal descent. I understand from our sages that a wormhole in time has opened for a short and maybe fleeting moment and that we now are able to communicate directly, however briefly. I have so much to say to you, but first I do hope you agree to talk to me, such an unknown entity, a kinsman maybe, but that far away.

SOLOMON: To say I am surprised is putting it very mildly; at first I thought I was dreaming. But whatever miracle this may be, let us use it to our advantage. First, knowing that my line still rules Israel is already a great boon, so please tell me more about yourself and the state of our realm, for it surely is ours jointly.

JOSIAH: I took the throne 360 years after you, as the nineteenth king of Judah. You were the third, so there are fifteen kings in between, starting with Rehoboam, your son by Naamah. First, maybe a deception for you: I am king of Judah and Benjamin, but not of the ten other tribes; immediately after your death the United Kingdom split, and Jeroboam—you surely know him, he is from Ephraim—took what is now called Israel.

SOLOMON: That is a pity, but it was to be expected, I guess. Those twelve tribes were an unruly lot to start with. My father David had already quite some trouble binding them together, and he was a most beloved and admired king. I did manage to keep the two parts united, but the fault lines were showing in my days already. Yes, I know Jeroboam, oh yes, I do know him, the son of Nebat, I chased him to Egypt.[1] But, maybe more importantly, how is Jerusalem doing, my city of cities? You still rule Judah from Jerusalem, do you?

JOSIAH: Sure, Jerusalem is doing fine, a great city, with even more people in it than in your times.[2] We are not as rich as you used to be, not by a far cry, but the city is still the stronghold of the covenant people, as well as a splendid defense against our enemies.

SOLOMON: Good to hear, though your mention of enemies is a little scary. Jerusalem is important, but the core of the city is my beloved temple, the one building that is so close to my heart: is it still standing? I aimed it to stand the onslaught of time, so did it?

JOSIAH: Yes it did, dear ancestor and great builder, it is still there. I am happy to report through this wonderful, almost divine, link my sages whipped up. The temple stands firm, in full splendor, as a fitting tribute to Yahweh.

SOLOMON: Great to know. How this would have warmed my father's heart who would so have liked to build such a shrine for the ark. The Lord did not let him, as he was too much of a warrior king, but he deeply loved the Lord. But tell me, what specifically did you want me to consult on?

JOSIAH: About history and the way to record it. Here at my court we are editing the history of Israel, and there you play a major part. So I take this miraculous opportunity to ask a major player in our great heritage to clarify some of the issues that befuddle us.

---

1. See 1 Kings 12:2.
2. There is a considerable debate regarding how large Jerusalem was during Solomon's reign. Strange enough, no traces have been found through archaeological research of any building associated with Solomon, but one has to bear in mind that excavation at the most relevant site, the Temple Mount, is impossible. So for the moment we only know of him through the Bible, and though many of the tales may well have been exaggerated—his riches and surely his number of wives—his historical existence is not in doubt. There is archaeological evidence for the "House of David," though. The same lack of external evidence holds, for that matter, for Josiah; he is also only known through the biblical account. His adversary, Necho II is definitely historical, part of the standard list of Egyptian Pharaohs.

SOLOMON: You are writing my history? How wonderful! What made you undertake such a great project?

JOSIAH: We have had a little bit too much of history, that is why. These 360 years between you and me have been a long time, and our history was not always gentle for the worship of Yahweh. Many kings have neglected the proper worship, put aside the successors of Zadok, and sacrificed for other gods, like Baal and Asherah. Even my grandfather Manasseh and my father Amon were more interested in their worship than in that of Yahweh, and the temple of the Lord has seen a lot of neglect, even outright abuse.

SOLOMON: I know about foreign gods, yes I do know, in my lifetime. So what did you do?

JOSIAH: Just a few years ago I decided to reinstate the temple, as it was a mess, so I ordered Hilkiah our high priest to cleanse it using some temple funds which still were there. And lo and behold, he showed up with what for him was a big surprise: a scroll, found in the wall of the temple.

SOLOMON: Much of the design of the temple came straight from the Lord, and my great architect Hiram followed these as far as specified. I do not remember anything about burying scrolls in the temple.

JOSIAH: I know you did not; it is a little complicated. I'll explain in a moment; bear with me. Anyway, we unrolled the document, priest Hilkiah read it aloud, and it turned out to be an account of Moses, with a major speech of his just before his death.

SOLOMON: We have several accounts of Moses in my court, but not with a major speech, as far as I can recall.

JOSIAH: No, the point is that this was an unknown piece, a second account of the law of Moses, beautifully written, elegant, and quite laudatory of the great Moses. I have used this new piece of the law to convince my people that we had to turn the tide of idolatry.

SOLOMON: How did you do it?

JOSIAH: I needed someone knowledgeable to tell the people that it was real. Our prophetess Huldah did that, and in no uncertain terms: this was the voice of the Lord speaking to us through that scroll.

SOLOMON: Parchment?

JOSIAH: No, papyrus. In front of all Jerusalem I then tore my clothes and declared that we had sinned, that we had to make a new covenant with the Lord, all of us, here and now.

SOLOMON: How did the people react?

JOSIAH: They were shocked and elated at the same time, shocked that the Lord had been forgotten this much and elated that he had spoken again, through written words. Just like the tables in the ark. I gave a speech, and we held a proper Pesach, the first correct and proper one in years. We had a great time and so did the priests and prophets.

SOLOMON: Prophets, plural?

JOSIAH: Yes we have three: Huldah, Jeremiah, and his old teacher Zephaniah.

SOLOMON: Hold on, this is a beautiful and inspiring story, but I am a king and not without some wisdom. Now you have me puzzled. You sent a major priest to cleanse the temple at the very moment the restorers happened to find the very scroll you needed, you chose a woman prophet while male prophets of repute were around, and your discovery nicely coincided with Pesach. I am a king, and you, dear grandson, seem to be a king as well, but if this was all by chance you would not be much of a king. No wise king would rely on so much coincidence—and you still are my progeny. Was it really an old scroll that you happened to find? Who made it, truly? What was behind it?

JOSIAH: I could have known that your wisdom would pierce through our pious charade.[3] Of course I knew about the scroll, and indeed I would be

---

3. I am following here scholarly consensus on the famous Josiah reform. His short reign (640–610 B.C.E.) has been of the utmost importance for the editing of the scriptures. The scroll in question usually is identified as a major part of Deuteronomy (literally: the Second Law), and though not undisputed, Jeremiah is

an inept king if such a document would have been developed without my knowledge. And the timing, well, you are right, we timed it meticulously. But it is the scroll that is important, and it was a cooperation between several people, prophets and scribes. Jeremiah was among them—he seems to have written a lot, Zephaniah probably, and others whose name would not mean anything to you. And, indeed, I chose Huldah because I could hardly ask the authors themselves, and she is of priestly family anyway. She was a safe bet.

SOLOMON: I thought so much, but is this the only scroll you have made?

JOSIAH: By no means. The making of the scroll is part of a much larger project, in which we are reworking all the materials we have. Part comes from your court—and thankful we are for your scribes! After the division of Israel, we have records from the Judean court, but also from the Northern Kingdom. Our people have been collecting them, also gathering some oral histories, putting all these records together as a whole.

SOLOMON: And they call me wise! I am so proud of you, seed of my seed. Now I understand what you said: you are editing the great tale of Israel, and, yes, I am proud that you do so, but what do you want to know of me?

---

mentioned as one of the possible authors. That Deuteronomy is not from the hand of Moses is crystal clear, but then scholarly consensus has it that none of the books of the Torah are. I follow here the almost classic Documentary Hypothesis, which has undergone significant modifications since its nineteenth-century inception, but still forms a major framework for constructing the writing and editing history of the Torah, the first five books of the Tanakh, the Jewish Bible, which Christians call the Old Testament. A recent alternative interpretation of the miraculous find of the scroll is as a metaphor for the whole Deuteronomist enterprise: the project to edit, harmonize, and integrate the texts and traditions of Israel, its history and its relation with Yahweh/Elohim. That does leave the authorship of the book of Deuteronomy open, however, as the origin of that fifth book of the Torah still falls, in all probability, in this same period. So I have followed the more established notion of a gentle charade by a king, who for both religious reasons and political expediency did away with all the other gods, killing quite a few of their priests, even going well beyond his territorial jurisdiction (see 2 Chronicles 34:4–7).

JOSIAH: I want to use this opportunity to solve a quandary we are in, and it is about you. You and your great father David—I am proud to count myself in his House[4]—form the high point in our history.

SOLOMON: Hard to disagree here.

JOSIAH: Your deep love for Yahweh shines through in the scattered documents we have from your court. You built the great temple we just cleansed, and we admire you for that; the temple is still called Solomon's temple.

SOLOMON: Wait, wait, it is the temple of Yahweh.

JOSIAH: Exactly. We have some of your words on record at inauguration of the temple, like this: "But will God really dwell on earth with humans? The heavens, even the highest heavens, cannot contain you. How much less this temple I have built! Yet, Lord my God, give attention to your servant's prayer and his plea for mercy. Hear the cry and the prayer that your servant is praying in your presence. . . . Hear from heaven, your dwelling place; and when you hear, forgive."[5] That is beautiful and so true.

SOLOMON: I vaguely remember saying things like that. Wonderful that you make it resonate again in the future.

JOSIAH: Thanks for your appreciation. On the other hand, however, we have records stating that you married many foreign women who followed their own religious customs. Is that correct?

SOLOMON: Yes, of course, that is what a king does. Most of the many women I married were for a large part political unions, and their kinsmen, important rulers at my borders, would have been severely insulted if I would not have humored their daughters in their sincere and noble worship of the gods of their fatherlands.[6]

---

4. Archeologists have found a seal with the inscription "House of David."

5. 2 Chronicles 6:18–21

6. Exclusivity in religious adherence is not a common element in religions at all and surely not in antique religions. Israel's religion is an exception in this matter. Solomon's argument, as constructed here, is politically sound and fits well in a multi-ethnic and multicultural realm. The biblical account devolves the guilt onto his wives, and indeed participation in sacrifices—the most common

JOSIAH: But some sources say you even joined them in their worship, that you "bowed before the foreign gods." If that is correct, how you could combine the worship of the Jerusalem temple with those of the other gods?

SOLOMON: In principle your record seems to be correct: I joined in with my wives. Being married to many women is not easy at all, you know, and one has to make accommodations. But, mark well in your records, that even when other gods vie for my attention, mainly through my wives, I never neglect Yahweh's temple here in Jerusalem. For instance, when I married Pharaoh's daughter, I lodged her in a house outside Zion, as that mountain was consecrated as the ark rested there.[7] My heart is with Yahweh, even if I join my wives in their particular sacrifices and prayers, and for Yahweh it is the heart that counts, I feel. Well, you seem to have me on the defensive now, just like some scribes here at court try to do. Oh, of course, you are citing them, I see.

JOSIAH: I personally have a problem with that, my dear Grandpa. My mother and the prophets always have taught me the Lord not only comes first, he also comes alone, and that Yahweh hated other gods. Was there no other way for you—did you have to be so lenient? You have a splendid reputation for wisdom—all sources testify to that. Is this wisdom?

SOLOMON: Well, yes, I gather wisdom comes in here. The worship of Yahweh is crucial for us, but for a king it has a different role than for a priest or for a peasant or soldier. I have a fairly large realm but constantly need allies against the larger powers, Assyria and Egypt. We made vassals of the Moabites, the Edomites, and even the Philistines, and Lebanon is our staunch ally. And these political unions come with respect for their gods as well. There should be some open competition for the favors of the various gods, with the king as the linchpin of power, arbitrator between the priests and mediator between the gods. It simply was my political realism that taught me as much. Indeed, wisdom.

---

form of ritual in all religions—is easy, as a sacrifice is in essence a joint meal aimed at uniting the partakers and the deity. But for a fairly large (how large is hard to establish) realm, an exclusive religion that does not proselyte offers poor prospects for integration. Even the Zoroastrian religion that formed the state religion of the Persians under Darius II was not that exclusive.

7. See 2 Chronicles 8:11.

JOSIAH: But I shudder at the sight and so do my prophets. My father Amon had left the temple as a rather run-down house of worship for many gods, with altars of Baal and poles of Asherah right inside the building.[8] These other gods not only had weeded over the temple, they do form an abomination to Yahweh. His words in this direction are crystal clear, at least for us: he will allow no other gods before our—and thus his—eyes.

SOLOMON: The temple of the Lord has to be his house exclusively, I concur on that. And I have to admit that some priests and scribes, as well as an occasional prophet, are starting to criticize me on my accommodation to my wives' gods, but that is their viewpoint as well as their interest.

JOSIAH: It is the Lord who speaks, I sincerely believe. When I came to the throne, still as a small boy, with the help of my mother and my counselors, we set out to throw out all that reeked after the foreign gods throughout the country, even in the land of Israel,[9] removing all traces of idolatry from my realm.

SOLOMON: That is your choice, and one I could not make. But, as you removed the other gods from "Eretz Israel," you surely also refurbished the other shrines of Yahweh in the land?

JOSIAH: They were in disarray, and I left them as I found them, for I want the temple to be the only place where one worships Yahweh, right here in Jerusalem. I feel that I really know that is what Yahweh wants from me.

SOLOMON: Was this really needed? I aimed the temple to be the first and foremost of all of Yahweh's places of worship; those in Carmel, Shiloh,

---

8. There are, actually, convincing reasons why Astarte or Asherah and Baal were that popular in Israel. Both deities were worshiped in the wide area—a much wider distribution than the cult of Yahweh ever had. They were primarily fertility gods, and their rituals occasionally involved a release of sexual mores. In this part of the Old Testament, one has to bear in mind, the "other gods" are still a theological reality. Till the Babylonian Exile, the God of Israel, according to his prophets, considers deities such as Baal and Asherah as competitors, as deities who "are there" but should not be followed. Only after the Babylonian episode do the texts attest a real monotheism, in which Yahweh/Elohim is the only existing deity, and mentioning or following other gods is an insult to the Lord—not because they exist but because believing in them detracts from the oneness and glory of God.

9. See 2 Chronicles 34:6, 7.

and Bethel have deeper roots in history of course, and surely Jerusalem should come first, but the only one? Of course, the temple of Yahweh has to outshine all shrines for other deities, even the ones I built for them.[10] In my view, having just one central shrine for Yahweh would not have been expedient. How could I rule a large kingdom with one bunch of priests only? In fact, the Zadokite priests would walk in too large shoes, having too much sway over the people.

JOSIAH: I am loath to admit that the other gods still are with us in the wide region. But I hate them and will not tolerate them in my country.

SOLOMON: But one is a king, and one has to think of the realm, keeping in view the larger picture. I never felt all my subjects would be able to live up to the stern commandments of Yahweh—for stern they are; you have to admit that.

JOSIAH: I beg to differ here. Yes, of course the service of Yahweh is never easy, and it was never intended to be so, but these rules both bind and protect the people. The central idea behind the temple always has been that of a covenant, going all the way back to Abraham, our apical ancestor.

SOLOMON: Wisdom, my dear descendant, wisdom is always needed. For a king there is always a political reality. That covenant is for Israel only and then quite demanding for many of them. My choice for leniency is part of the reality of my realm, and I can see that your situation is different; my borders are much farther from Jerusalem and quite secure.

JOSIAH: Sorry, Grandpa, I did not mean to criticize you, but I get quite emotional over these other gods. Yes, my kingdom now is much smaller than yours and your divide and rule policy would not work in our small realm. We need our people to focus just on Jerusalem and have an undivided loyalty towards our kingdom, to me, and most assuredly to Yahweh. So one temple for Yahweh in my realm, no other shrines for our Lord, and surely no sacred sites for the other gods is what suits our situation best. But I really believe Yahweh wants it!

SOLOMON: I know you do. The overall political situation has been favorable for my father and me, as the great powers were in tatters at the

10. See 1 Kings 11:4.

time when Samuel made Saul into the first king. Compared to Assyria and Egypt we still are small, but the last century they have been recovering from severe set-backs,[11] which gives us breathing space. But still, I do have to deal with peoples on my borders, and they all have their own gods with their weird cults. Luckily, they also have daughters, and are they beautiful! How is your overall political situation?

JOSIAH: We are in a squeeze, actually, by the great powers. Egypt is strong, Assyria is dangerous, and we are more or less the highway that connects them—very uncomfortable. They are surely infringing upon us. Some forty-four years ago the kingdom of Israel fell, overrun by Assur. King Nebuchadnezzar sacked Israel's cities, destroyed the temples you mentioned in Carmel, Hebron, Bethel, and Shiloh, and destroyed our brothers. They even took a lot of them captive and have transported them somewhere else. The land lies waste now, and we have no clue where these ten tribes went, somewhere up north. Nobody has heard of them any-more; they might be up in the northern ranges of the Assur kingdom, but who knows the limits of that realm?

SOLOMON: That is sad news, really sad. It breaks my heart. I never would have thought our kingdom would end that badly; those beautiful lands laid waste, the people led away to the heathen lands beyond the horizon, what a shame. How could this happen? How could the Lord allow this to happen? Ours never has been a great realm, not compared to Egypt, Persia, Babylon, or Assur, but we hold our own. And surely we have the Lord on our side, so what happened?

JOSIAH: That is the main question. Why did the Lord forsake them— and consequently, will he forsake us? Between your realm and my king-dom we saw a lot of prophets, who zoomed in on this question. You had some in your time—

SOLOMON: Yes, and a botheration they are! Never content, always know-ing better, and ever at odds with the priests themselves. Though, they were well pleased with the temple when it was finished, I have to say that. But no respect for the king whatsoever. Father David had a clash with Nathan

---

11. The thirteenth and twelfth centuries B.C.E. formed the stage of the so-called Bronze Age collapse, when the old bronze-based polities fell under environmental pressures, giving way to the later Iron Age kingdoms, to which Solomon's realm belonged.

over my dear mother, mind you![12] In other kingdoms people with such a message would not live long, just thanks to their direct link with Yahweh that they are still around.

JOSIAH: We read about your mother's story! I gather it has been hard for you, but I rely on prophets quite a bit, though. In fact, I think I could not be king without them.

SOLOMON: They try to forbid me three things: horses, gold, and wives. How can a king go without these three? From Saul onward, Israel liked to have a king, but still does not like their king to really behave like one. And the prophets lead them in that sentiment. By the way, you do realize that some are impostors, and just a few are the real deal; actually, the latter ones are hard to handle, the first ones just say what I like to hear. Difficult, for a king.[13]

JOSIAH: That has changed; people now accept kingly behavior. Those prophets, the prophets of the Lord that is, what you call the real deal,[14] became more numerous, and more vocal, at both the courts of Judah and Israel.[15] The point is that some kings listen and some don't, especially those of Israel hardly paid any attention to them. That is why, we think, Israel has been lost: on the whole, it left the service of Yahweh, and Yahweh has punished it. The gods of your wives might have been expedient for you, but our scribes think in the end they undid the kingdom. Taking in other gods was, many here at court feel, a dangerous path. So it is our deep conviction that even if we cannot turn the course of history, we have

---

12. See 2 Samuel 12:1–6.

13. This may sound surprising, but the relative freedom and—also relative—immunity of prophets from violent reactions of the kings is a distinguishing feature of Israel's prophetism. That does not mean that the prophets did not suffer at the hands of kings—they surely did—but viewing the liberties the prophets took in chastising strong kings, the prophetic life expectancy could have been much shorter than it seemed to have been.

14. The institution of prophethood was complicated in Israel. There must have been schools of prophets, like the ones that Saul encountered, and throughout the prophetic period (see next note) a distinction between prophets and prophet-of-the-Lord was made.

15. The period between 800 and 300 B.C.E. has been characterized as the prophetic period in Israel's history, ending, indeed, with Malachi. It roughly coincides with what is now called the Axial Age, the birth period of world religions.

to go back to the covenant, back to the temple, and we should do this completely, holding back nothing: surely no other gods, but also no other shrines for Yahweh in the region. We put our faith in Jerusalem as the seat of the Lord; that way we may survive the onslaught of the great powers. And coming back to our quest, because of this threat from outside, we embarked on this journey to collate all the histories of Israel and Judah. And you were there, at a crucial cusp in time.

SOLOMON: I now understand your quandary, dear and faithful descendant: your real problem is how to depict me: as a wise and pious king of Israel or as someone who led the nation on a dangerous path. Is that it?

JOSIAH: I am glad you put it this clearly, for it is not up to me to judge my ancestor. But my editing team is struggling over this question.

SOLOMON: I see the issue, at least for your team. And of course I am concerned how I will go down in history—you seem to hold the keys to my reputation! So, for the records: be convinced that I deeply love Yahweh, and I would have loved to be able to limit myself just to his service. But wisdom—I am glad that fame survived—dictated otherwise, political wisdom. So I might be both the wise king as well as the mistaken one. Maybe eradicating the other gods would have changed the course of history or the future; they seem to mingle here. Who knows? But deeper wisdom dictates that one does not speculate about the future and surely not about alternative futures—that would really be vanity of vanities. So please leave it in the final records in this way: I have my strong and weak points and what is strong and what is weak—let history decide. And that history surely will not end in your era so just record it both ways.

JOSIAH: I bow for your wisdom, dear Grandpa. We will be as honest as we can, for though we are writing about history, the records are for the future. I consider our project as a link in a noble chain—the preservation of the word.

SOLOMON: Here we agree again: it is all about preserving the Word of God. The temple is the abode of the ark, and the ark a chest for the Word. My foreign wives sometimes chide me that our temple is empty, without a statue of the god. And what strange god would forbid his own statue? Then I try to explain that the temple enshrines the ten commandments and thus the word of Yahweh. That is difficult for them. So tell me: is the ark still in the temple?

JOSIAH: Yes, we recently put it back in,[16] and the tables are still there. I do hope they will be forever.

SOLOMON: But your project does more than just record history: it also lays down the Word. So in your time there are two sets of words: the tables and your scrolls. That means you do not only save the temple, but you also give the words of God a double security. Well, this may come as a surprise to you, but the ark itself is also doubled.

JOSIAH: Yes, that is a surprise. How? And where is that second ark?

SOLOMON: I do hope you have in your records the story of the visit of the queen of Sheba.

JOSIAH: Yes, we have it on record, an exciting episode.

SOLOMON: It was indeed. We had a good time, and she went home pregnant.[17] As a parting gift I had a copy of the ark made for her, with copies of the tables as well. As far as I know they arrived safe in Sheba, where she gave birth to a son, Menelik. I hope and trust that they will guard their ark just as well as you have done. It must be somewhere in their lands, deep in the south, far away.

---

16. Where the ark had been stored is not exactly clear from the text. It is usually surmised that Manasseh, with his devotion to Baal and Asherah, had the ark removed from the temple, but the text is not definitive about this. In I Chronicles 35:3 Josiah orders the Levites to put the ark back into the temple, instead of carrying on their shoulders, but that begs the question.

17. I am following here a persistent and old Ethiopian tradition, that their dynasty stems from Solomon, through the visit of the Queen. Also the presence of an ark—or for the Ethiopians the ark—is the topic of a widespread story; it would have been kept in a monastery in Axum, belonging to the Church of Our Lady Mary of Zion, where it reputedly still is. Its presence has never been affirmed by the Ethiopian government, nor, for that matter, denied. The link between Israel and Ethiopia is strong, including the presence of Jews in Ethiopia, who migrated to Israel in great numbers in the 1970s. So, though speculative, the story is not without its foundation.

JOSIAH: It seems our line is folding, the wormhole—whatever that may be—seems spent. I have to go off to block the way of the Pharaoh Necho II, in order for him not to reach Assur.[18] I go to the battle with a happy heart, knowing that the fate of the word is secure.[19]

SOLOMON: Thanks for calling upon me, my dear descend—

---

18. This was not a wise move, neither politically nor from a military point of view. Pharaoh Necho II had no issue with Josiah, and he told the king as much (see 2 Chronicles 35:21). Also his prophets were not too happy about it, especially Jeremiah. Josiah did engage the troops of Pharaoh and, almost inevitably, lost. Why Josiah did this is not clear; maybe he thought that Assur would be grateful for keeping Necho out of their braided hair and thus spare him the fate of the Northern Kingdom. But it is during this period that Babylon would topple Assyria and come over and finish the subjugation of the small Judean kingdom, leading to the Babylonian captivity. Anyway, Josiah was no match for Necho II and was killed; the details are in 2 Chronicles 35:22–24. For Jeremiah this must have been devastating, and his Lamentations testify as much. Few prophets have written so much in and of the Bible as this prophet.

19. The second major phase of scripture editing and writing came during the Babylonian Exile, as well as just after it, when the first exiles came home, including Ezra and Nehemiah.

Jeremiah and Jonah: Doom and Deliverance

Walter E. A. van Beek

JONAH: Dear Jeremiah, let me first state that I have nothing but the deepest respect for you. You are one of those prophets of the Gods that I try to emulate. I write you to state this, but also to tell you that we have been much closer connected than you may know: I have been inside you! I spent three days inside a huge fish—you may have heard of the story—and that fish, I learned later, had a name, yours: Jeremiah![1] At the time I was glad to say farewell to the beast but it seems that, according to some colleague prophets of ours, we—meaning the fish and me—will be re-awakened, as they call it, after the destruction of Jerusalem. And that is where you come in again, for that destruction is very much your personal arena with Yahweh. Maybe we can share experiences about Yahweh, our god, as I am not very content in his service, and I understand that you have a lot to complain about as well.

JEREMIAH: Good to hear from you, dear colleague; I never knew that fishes had names, surely not mine. Poor fish to bear a name that has become an omen of suffering and lament. Yes, I had my share of mishaps in my life, but never by an animal. With me, it was the priests of Yahweh, who had me beaten and put into jail, or Zedekiah's counselors dropping me in a cistern.[2] If it were not for the Babylonians I would not be alive today, as they have been nothing but kind to me, and if my present king had not panicked and fled to exile in Egypt,[3] I would still be enjoying their

---

1. In a richly illustrated sixteenth-century manuscript called the *Zubdat-al Tawarikh*, Jonah is portrayed with "his" fish Jeremiah, just after their reawakening in the Uzeyr wilderness. The manuscript is dedicated to Sultan Murad III, in 1583, and resides in the Museum of Turkish and Islamic Arts in Istanbul.

2. Jeremiah 20:1–4, 38:6, 28. See also Jeremiah 11:18–23.

3. See Jeremiah 43.

esteem. It seems that for both of us, our help comes from the outside more than from the covenant people. With you it was Nineveh, I heard?

JONAH: Yes, Yahweh called me to Nineveh because he wanted to destroy that wicked city.[4] I did not want to go, actually, but wound up there anyway. Thanks to "Jeremiah," my fish, that is. He gobbled me up after the sailors threw me overboard, and spit me out on land. So I had to go to Nineveh willy-nilly. Actually, once I was in Nineveh, I rather liked the idea that they would get their well-deserved punishment, their comeuppance, so I tried to do a good job, preaching their doom. That is what you have been doing most of your life, haven't you?

JEREMIAH: Yes, in Jerusalem mainly, and now in Egypt. It started out so well, with the wonderful reform of Josiah after he found the scroll in the temple.[5] The whole nation repented, it was great, and we had the first proper Pesach feast since ages. Of course that scroll helped, and I did have some hand in that, but our young king picked it up wonderfully, and the time seemed so bright. Too bad he tried to block the armies of Pharaoh, and was killed. He had just turned forty, though I did write a nice lament for him. Since then, it was all downhill, those kings never listen, do they?

JONAH: Well, mine did in fact, the one in Nineveh, he did listen, came from his throne, sat on the floor, and made the whole city repent. Even the animals![6] Even they had to fast, you wouldn't believe it! Well, my life keeps being intertwined with beasts. But I was angry at Yahweh, for he spared

---

4. As far as historicity is concerned, the Book of Jonah is among the least historic tales in the Bible. The Jonah figure in the Book of Jonah has probably nothing to do with the prophet Jonah mentioned in 2 Kings 14:25, during the reign of Jeroboam (748–728 B.C.E.). The dating of the Book of Jonah is difficult—Persia appears in the Israelite record only after the Babylonian captivity, and thus it may have been written between the fifth and the third century. Viewing the long and intricate string of improbabilities in the tale, with miracles that even seem quite pointless, a plausible interpretation is that the book is a satire, ridiculing prophetic schools that deemed themselves the cream of society, self-indulgent and pompous, instead of really following the Lord. In my treatment I take the story as a given, ignoring the satire, to highlight the main message of the text itself.

5. See 2 Kings 22–24 and 2 Chronicles 34–35. See also my dialogue between Josiah and Solomon in this volume.

6. They are indeed explicitly mentioned in the Book of Jonah, several times, reinforcing the satirical element of the book.

the city, tenderhearted as he sometimes is, and forgave the people their sins. I must say they did put up a good show, especially when the animals wore a mourning shroud, but I expected the Lord to be just, and mete out justice, well-deserved, quick and severe. But no, he accepted their repentance, and they all lived, mind you. Those people were wicked, whatever they said when I was there. It is not right: the just should be rewarded, and the wicked punished, that is how life should be. Down with Nineveh and down with its people. And Yahweh should know that.

JEREMIAH: Well, I wish I could have had your astonishing success, especially after Josiah died. I preached my whole life to the people of Judah, and I got nowhere. In the end the Babylonians came in, took Jerusalem, and did destroy the temple. As I said, they respected me more than my own people did. If it were not for my friends and Baruch, my pupil, my life would have been much shorter and quite useless.

JONAH: At least you witnessed that the destruction you predicted came about, that is quite gratifying, isn't it?

JEREMIAH: I am not so sure. Yes, I preached repentance to the people, and yes, I predicted the destruction of the temple, but the idea was that they should repent. Actually, I did not want the temple to be destroyed and surely not my very own people. They were angry, all right, and wanted to kill me, but they still somewhere respected my calling and let me go. Too bad that did not hold for my colleague Uriah; maybe he should not have panicked.[7] Anyway, I feel I am called to preach repentance, not doom. The point is that people have to choose themselves for or against Yahweh. Even if the covenant was collective, the one we orchestrated with king Josiah, each person has to decide for his own; that is what the Lord had me proclaim at the steps of the temple.[8] The priests were furious because I put the temple in jeopardy, while the king thought his people should simply follow his lead; he already was not too pleased when I compared him and his retinue with rotten figs. I lost on both ends. Still, I deeply believe that people can change their hearts.

---

7. The prophet Uriah fled from Jehoiakim, king of Judah, to Egypt, but was routed, brought back to Jerusalem and beheaded: see Jeremiah 26:20–23.

8. The so-called Temple Sermon; see Jeremiah 28.

JONAH: No, people are what they are, bound to obedience or destruction. The world needs to be a sure place, with clear rules, and swift punishment, not the wishy-washy of a little bit of good that annuls a lot of evil. The scales of justice should prevail, not the weeping heart of compassion. Actually, Yahweh in the past was very good in punishment, remember the Amalekites who were not even allowed to exist; but just when one settles down in a nice routine of rewarding the just and obliterating the wicked, he comes along and forgives a whole city. And even one that takes three days to pass through—it would have been such a good example for the whole world, better even than Gomorrah. The world needs examples, not forgiveness, the Lord has to be feared.

JEREMIAH: Maybe some fear might help, but that angle did not work with me. However, even when the Lord says he will send in his wrath, he always promises great things for the faithful after final deliverance. For him, there is always an open door, even at the end of a very long hallway. He calls, sometimes shouts, or cajoles, but always in order to have people change their ways. You should be proud of Nineveh.

JONAH: Well, Yahweh went to some length to teach me as much, with that miracle tree. At last I had some shade, given by him, and he took it away. But maybe people are more important than a bit of shade for a lonely prophet, maybe he was right. I felt like I was the laughing stock in Nineveh, and I do not like to play the fool. I am important, for I am the prophet of Yahweh, and that should be respected. Clearly, I was right from the start: I did not want to become a prophet in the first place. I tried my utmost to escape the call.

JEREMIAH: There we have a clear understanding, my friend. I struggled against my call as well,[9] like Moses did, trying to find all kind of excuses: too young, not good at speaking, afraid of people. But he said he knew me from before my birth, and I had to do it. Besides, when I tried not to speak the word of the Lord, they became like burning fire inside me. I could not hold them.[10] Only when I spoke these words, my mouth cooled.

JONAH: I tried to run, as fast and as far as I could, you know the story. He called me to the east, so I took a westbound ship, that would do the

9. Jeremiah 20:7.
10. Jeremiah 20:9.

trick I thought. But no, he sends a storm and has the dice show the sailors that I was to blame. And, mind you, they respected my prophetic calling more than I did; they even tried to save my life by rowing against the storm. In the end they did throw me overboard, as I had suggested as a final way to escape from Yahweh. But then that darned fish—sorry, Jeremiah—came along, gobbled me up, and after three days threw me up on the beach. Well, I did learn to pray inside that fish, and from then I did what the Lord told me to do. So maybe it is right and fitting that it has your name.

JEREMIAH: OK, if that is the case, I take honor in having a fish named after me, also a proper reflection of my pitiful circumstances here in Egypt. But we do agree on one thing: being called as a prophet is not a good career choice. Just living a life of a priest, like my father, is much more gratifying. Throughout my life I have struggled with my calling, but Yahweh simply was too strong for me, so I had to go out and preach. Those false prophets have a cushy career, saying what people like to hear, but for us there was no rest, no respite, and surely no respect from our own people. You had foreign sailors who understood your calling, I had a Chushite saving me, you had Persians repenting, I had Babylonians honoring me.[11]

JONAH: Yes, with Yahweh you can expect the unexpected. My name has become a buzzword among sailors for someone who brings bad luck, while I was saved by the strangest of miracles. In the end, looking back upon it, the whole event seemed hazy, like a dream of old, but that fish at least will never be forgotten.

JEREMIAH: I often wondered whether your story in fact was not a dream, more than actual history. As you may know, Tobit, the pious Jew from Nineveh, praised the Lord for dealing harshly with both Babylon and Nineveh, glad he had witnessed the destruction of that city before he died.[12] Not everyone takes his account seriously, but it does contradict your story. Maybe it was all a dream, who knows.

JONAH: Sometimes I wonder whether I really lived through that journey; in fact I hope it was all a dream. I am an extremely pleasant guy, but I come out as headstrong, petulant, and vindictive. I will not take

11. See Jeremiah 38.
12. See Tobit 14:15.

that! Maybe obedience and longsuffering forms the usual job profile for a prophet, but not for me. Anyway, whether the experience was a dream or not, one thing shines through: once the Lord has called you, there is little you can do to thwart him and definitely do not expect an easy life. I ran from my calling, and maybe you should have done as well. You have had your troubles, I heard, you were not allowed to marry or to have kids, could never go to a wedding or a funeral, or even any feast. What kind of a life is that?

JEREMIAH: The Lord sometimes seems to have his own reasons, and suffering is always part of these. I lived in "interesting times" and thus had an "interesting life," too much so in fact. I am sorry that I happened to be the prophet of Yahweh in this cusp of time, but it is his work, not necessarily my life, that counts.

JONAH: In the end one has to ask: A life with all those sacrifices, is it really worth it?

JEREMIAH: It is the legacy that counts more than an easy life. I did speak for the Lord. I could dictate his words in several books, one of which generated a major reform, and even when I lamented the fate of Jerusalem, I felt part of a deep, venerated history, part of the work of the Lord.

JONAH: I am glad to hear that Nineveh is destroyed after all. They had it coming. That sham conversion! Now that Jerusalem also is destroyed, maybe I will be reunited with that fish, your namesake. Not a pleasant future, but it seems to be all I have. What do you look forward to?

JEREMIAH: Despite being all gloom at the moment, I keep looking forward to the long, glorious future that the Lord has been promising that since ages. The land of Israel will be redeemed, Jerusalem will be rebuilt, the temple restored, and there we all will meet, priests, princes, peasants, and prophets. So, cheer up my friend, till we meet in Jerusalem, till we meet in Jerusalem.

Hannah and Sariah: Complaint

Miranda Wilcox

Hannah lived in Ramahaim-zophim in the mountains of Ephraim in mid-eleventh century B.C. at the end of the reign of judges. Sariah lived in Jerusalem in the sixth century B.C.E. at the eve of the Babylonian captivity. The stories of both women highlight their pivotal roles in significant political and religious transitions in ancient Israel. Canonized scriptural records preserve their prayers of complaint and of thanksgiving as they consecrate themselves to God's work by dedicating their families to the revolutionary prophetic careers of their sons and husband. In addition, both women manifest piety and compel God's response through personal prayer and by participating in cultic worship practices. Their ability to innovate private communication with God within institutional structures controlled by religious and social authorities—priests and husbands—reveals glimpses of largely undocumented female spiritual experiences.

The narrative of 1 Samuel portrays the birth of Hannah's son as a significant factor in the transformation of the political and religious institutions of Israel between 1050 and 1000 B.C.E. The books of Nephi trace how Lehi and Sariah's family found a new Israelite community in the Americas in the seventh century B.C.E.

Shiloh and Jerusalem were both major cultic centers of the periods. Hannah and her family (husband Elkanah and his wife Peninnah and their children) traveled to Shiloh once a year to offer sacrifices at the sanctuary in Shiloh that housed the Ark of the Covenant. However, the shrine in Shiloh in the pre-monarchic period was vulnerable: the chief priest's family was cursed for their corruption, and invading Philistines stole the Ark of the Covenant. As a priest, judge, and prophet, Samuel was a key figure in keeping the Israelites' religious heritage and identity alive during Israel's defeat and occupation by the Philistines, and at the end of his life he anointed the monarchs Saul and David who unified the disparate tribes of Israel into a kingdom and minor Palestinian empire.

About 600 B.C.E., the prophet Jeremiah warned the inhabitants of Judah and Jerusalem that their holy city, Jerusalem, like Shiloh, would be ruined.[1] Lehi, Sariah's husband, joined the group of prophets preaching repentance in Jerusalem, and when his life was threatened their family left Jerusalem. En-route to the American continent they melded their familial cultic practices from Jerusalem with revelations about the advent of Christ into a proto-Christianity.

I imagine a conversation between Hannah and Sariah in post-mortality after they read the canonized scriptural accounts of their respective families. Although both women have cause to say as does the personified scriptural Zion, "The Lord has forsaken me, my Lord has forgotten me,"[2] they both witness that God promises women, "For a small moment have I forgotten thee; but with great mercies will I gather thee."[3]

Complaint characterizes the voices of Hannah and Sariah in the scriptural record. Hannah explains her tearful prayer to Eli, "for out of the abundance of my complaint and grief have I spoken hitherto."[4] Nephi characterizes his mother's reaction to her sons' return to Jerusalem, "and after this manner of language had my mother complained against my father."[5] Some contemporary readers have criticized Hannah and Sariah for complaining without appreciating the meaning of the term "complain" or the ancient complaint genre. The modern English word "complain" derives from the intensified form of the Latin verb *plangere,* "to lament, bewail," originally "to strike, beat, beat the breast or head in sign of grief." The primary definition of complain in the Oxford English Dictionary is "to give expression to sorrow or suffering." In the scriptures, complaints invite God to respond with compassion and mercy. These women do not rebelliously murmur; they acknowledge the painful stakes in their faith.

* * * * * * *

HANNAH: Welcome Sariah, matriarch of Israel in the New World.

SARIAH: Greetings Hannah, mother of the founder of the Kingdom of Israel.

---

1. See Jeremiah 7:12–15 and 26:5–9.
2. Isaiah 49:14.
3. Isaiah 54:7.
4. 1 Samuel 1:16.
5. 1 Nephi 5:3.

HANNAH: Motherhood is the heart of our honor and sorrow.

SARIAH: Indeed, Eve's legacy to her daughters.

HANNAH: A legacy I feared had been thwarted; no seed swelled in my womb, no milk flowed from my breast until Samuel.

SARIAH: Did the Lord demand that you sacrifice your child, the fruit of your long barren womb, back to Him as He did Abraham and Sarah?

HANNAH: No longer could I endure the pity of Elkanah and the taunts of Peninnah. Elkanah tried to console me with his favor, but my barrenness shamed me, isolated me, amid Peninnah's children. How could he love me as he said I should love him? I was no better to him than ten sons. Was I so ungrateful to want a son?

SARIAH: Is a woman's worth based on the children she bears?

HANNAH: It is evident in the portions of the sacrificial offerings that Elkanah gave his wives. A woman is destitute if her husband dies before she has children.

SARIAH: True.

HANNAH: On the steps of the sanctuary in Shiloh, I poured out my soul unto the Lord. My hunger for a child gnawed my soul in bitterness, my tears emptied my heart, my lips moved in silent plea that the Lord might rain forth fertile waters on my dry roots. I had only hope to sacrifice, so I pledged to return the Lord's gift of a son to Him.

SARIAH: I was not so generous when God laid claim to my sons. My husband dreamed that the Lord commanded my sons to return to Jerusalem to obtain the records of our forefathers from our powerful kinsman Laban. Such a journey was certain death; they would perish in the wilderness. Their sun-bleached bones scavenged by beasts and buried in the sand haunted me. When my youngest son Nephi said that the Lord would prepare a way for this hard thing, I wept. Whence comes such faith? Obedience incises reason and love; it rent my soul.

HANNAH: Who understands what the Lord gives and takes away?

SARIAH: Hannah, why did you go to the temple to plead with the Lord? Did the Lord answer your prayer there? When my four sons left our camp, I leaned against the altar of stones my husband erected in the desert where we had offered thanksgiving for our lives. But I saw only the glint of a thief's dagger, heard the bark of a jackal, thirsted for a pool of water, and feared the murderous rage of Laban. Could God hear my prayers a three-day journey from the temple in Jerusalem?

HANNAH: God directed Abraham to travel three days to Moriah to make a burnt offering.

SARIAH: Sarah was left behind.

HANNAH: Do you think she knew why her husband took Isaac to worship with him?

SARIAH: Maybe she laughed.

HANNAH: I did not hear a voice from the Ark of God. My son would hear Him there; three times the voice of God would wake Samuel. Would I have answered as humbly if God had called, "Hannah"? Would His voice have pierced my grief and shame? The priest Eli interrupted my prayer to accuse me of being drunk. Could he not see I was pouring out sorrow not wine?

SARIAH: Do you believe Eli when he said God would grant your petition? Eli's priestly line was failing—his sons would be slain and the Ark taken by the Philistines not many years later.

HANNAH: His words eased the flood of pain. Maybe I was desperate for some divine acknowledgment. Eli was inept and his words unsatisfying, but they sealed my covenant. Neither of us knew that my son would replace his sons. I had heard rumors about Eli's sons, but if I had known how degenerate they were, I would never have exposed my son to their perversions of the priestly office. At least Eli kept Samuel close and taught him to recognize God's voice. God tutored Samuel; Samuel tutored Israel.

SARIAH: God tutored Lehi and Nephi; they tutored the family.

HANNAH: Even in your sorrow after your sons departed for Jerusalem?

SARIAH: Lehi testified that he was a visionary man and knew the goodness of God. What comfort is a land of promise if we were alone? I trusted my husband when he came home talking about visions and dreams. I comforted him when street crowds jeered at his prophesies. I did not try to dissuade him from preaching even when they sought to take away his life. To save him, I packed our household onto backs of camels and traveled into the wilderness. I left my home, my parents, and my daughters with their husbands' families in Jerusalem. Under the hot sun, I tried to soothe my sons' fears and doubts about their father's dangerous plans. Yet when I pleaded with God to understand His will for my family, silence echoed from the altar of stones in the desert. How quickly God visited Nephi when he sought to know His dealings with his father.

HANNAH: Does God speak to women?

SARIAH: He wrenches our hearts and our loins. I would be a barren woman bereft of children—my daughters lost in captivity and my sons perished in the wilderness. Bitterness twisted my heart already bruised with sorrow. Was this God's tender mercy or Lehi's foolish imagination?

HANNAH: It is so difficult to discern.

SARIAH: Not until I saw my sons' heads crest the horizon was I comforted. Then I knew of a surety of the Lord's deliverance. I sang a prayer of thanksgiving; we offered sacrifices and burnt offerings to the Lord. But the joy of my sons' return was the only glimpse I had of what it would be like to taste the white fruit on the tree in Lehi's and Nephi's dreams, for the taste of salvation is reunion and reconciliation. Such sweetness soon turned bitter as my sons feuded; there would be no resolution between Laban's and Lemuel's steadfast inflexibility in their loyalty to traditions of Jerusalem and Nephi's arrogant judgment in his precocious visionary gift.

HANNAH: Sorrow always tempers joy. God gave me the perfect gift. As Samuel nuzzled my breast, I wondered how I could give him up. No one would love him as I loved him. But when he was weaned, I took him and three bullocks, flour, and wine to the house of the Lord in Shiloh.

SARIAH: No angel stayed your hand? No ram appeared in the thicket?

HANNAH: The priests killed a bullock and took my child. What kind of mother gives away her child, like an animal?

SARIAH: What kind of God lets her?

HANNAH: I covenanted that I would lend him to the Lord, as the Lord lent him to me. Alone on the temple steps once more, I saw the Lord's face and sang a new song. We fulfilled our covenant! He would fulfill His covenant with Israel, and Samuel would play a role in reversing Israel's fortunes.

SARIAH: God is merciful. He sent me Jacob, Joseph, Elisheba, and Tirzah as peaceful balm while we traversed continents and oceans amid their brothers' quarrels. They did not resent the hardships of our journey; Jerusalem did not haunt them as it did the rest of us.

HANNAH: Praise the Lord, for his mercy endures forever. Every year I made Samuel a cloak to wear with his priestly ephod, and God filled my arms with sons and daughters. No longer was I barren, though Samuel was not mine to raise.

HANNAH and SARIAH: Let us approach the throne of God and sing a song of thanksgiving:

> Answer me when I call, O God of my right!
>> Thou hast given me room when I was in distress.
>> Be gracious to me, and hear my prayer.
> O men, how long shall my honor suffer shame?
>> How long will you love vain words, and seek after lies? *Selah*
>> But know that the Lord has set apart the godly for himself;
>> the Lord hears when I call to him.
> Be angry, but sin not;
>> commune with your own hearts on your beds, and be silent.
>> *Selah*
>> Offer right sacrifices,
>> and put your trust in the Lord.
> There are many who say, "O that we might see some good!
>> Lift up the light of thy countenance upon us, O Lord!"

Thou hast put more joy in my heart
than they have when their grain and wine abound.
In peace I will both lie down and sleep;
for thou alone, O Lord, makest me dwell in safety.[6]

We had thought this was Hannah's song about her son. It is. It concerns her "horn." The song, however breaks out beyond Hannah. It now trusts in and anticipates the "horn of David," who is the true horn of Israel. It anticipates that Yahweh will reorder social reality, precisely in the interest of those too poor and too weak to make their own way. . . . This song provides an "interpretive key" for the books of Samuel. That is, the power and willingness of Yahweh to intrude, intervene, and invert is the main theme of this narrative. We watch while the despised ones (Israel, David) become great ones. . . .

This song becomes the song of Mary and the song of the church (Luke 1:46–55), as the faithful community finds in Jesus the means through which Yahweh will turn and right the world. The Song of Mary, derived from Hannah, becomes the source for Luke's radical portrayal of Jesus. This song becomes a source of deep and dangerous hope in the world wherever the prospect and possibility of human arrangements have been exhausted. When people can no longer believe the promises of the rulers of this age, when the gifts of well-being are no longer given through established channels, this song voices an alternative to which the desperate faithful cling.

First Samuel 2:1–10 begins in barrenness redeemed; barrenness, however, is the penultimate humiliation. The last threat is death and the best, most astonishing gift is resurrection life. Hannah and Israel sing of the one who "brings to life," who breaks the power of death. It does not matter that power is experienced as barrenness, as despair, or as oppression. Hannah flings this song buoyantly in the face of the power of death. Her act is an act of daring hope, rooted in a concrete gift, waiting for more of life yet to be given. Our interpretive responsibility now is to see who among us can join this dangerous, daring song to this same God who has power to transform and willingness to intervene. That power to transform and willingness are the source of Israel's only consolation (Luke 2:25) and are the energy that drives Samuel's narrative to its remarkable Davidic possibility.

Walter Brueggemann, *First and Second Samuel*, 20–21.

---

6. Psalm 4 (RSV).

ISAIAH 54 (3 NEPHI 22)

1. Sing, O barren, thou that didst not bear; break forth into singing, and cry aloud, thou that didst not travail with child: for more are the children of the desolate than the children of the married wife, saith the Lord.

2. Enlarge the place of thy tent, and let them stretch forth the curtains of thine habitations: spare not, lengthen thy cords, and strengthen thy stakes;

3. For thou shalt break forth on the right hand and on the left; and thy seed shall inherit the Gentiles, and make the desolate cities to be inhabited.

4. Fear not; for thou shalt not be ashamed; neither be thou confounded; for thou shalt not be put to shame: for thou shalt forget the shame of thy youth, and shalt not remember the reproach of thy widowhood any more.

5. For thy Maker is thy husband; the Lord of hosts is his name; and thy Redeemer the Holy One of Israel; the God of the whole earth shall he be called.

6. For the Lord hath called thee as a woman forsaken and grieved in spirit, and a wife of youth, when thou wast refused, saith thy God.

7. For a small moment have I forgotten thee; but with great mercies will I gather thee.

8. In a little wrath I hid my face from thee for a moment; but with everlasting kindness will I have mercy on thee, saith the Lord thy Redeemer.

10. For the mountains shall depart and the hills be removed; but my kindness shall not depart from thee, neither shall the covenant of my peace be removed, saith the Lord that hath mercy on thee.

13. And all thy children shall be taught of the Lord; and great shall be the peace of thy children.

Biblical scholars recognize the theological significance of juxtaposing lament and praise, particularly in the psalms. Influenced by liberation theologian Dorothee Soelle, who said that "to deal with suffering, we need theological hope, which connects our pain with the pain of God," Walter Brueggemann argues that "suffering in Israel (voiced as complaint) turns out to be the candid arena for hope (voiced as praise)," and that "these moments of candor, communion, and gratitude are the demanding road" of an authentic life of faith.[7]

---

7. Dorothee Soelle, "God's Pain and Our Pain," in *The Future of Liberation Theology: Essays in Honor of Gustavo Gutiérrez*, ed. Marc H. Ellis and Otto Maduro (Maryknoll, N.Y.: Orbis Books, 1989), 332. Walter Brueggemann, *The Psalms and the Life of Faith* (Minneapolis: Fortress Press, 1995), 212. See also Claus Westermann, *Praise and Lament in the Psalms* (Louisville: John Knox Press, 1981), and Miriam J. Bier and Tim Bulkeley, eds., *Spiritual Complaint: The Theology and Practice of Lament* (Cambridge: James Clark, 2014).

Hannah and Sariah legitimate a sequence of complaint and praise as a means of authentically communicating with God. Too often public worship bleaches suffering thereby depriving worshippers of a liturgical form with sufficient emotional depth to resonate with human reality. May we share our pain and hope in worship through complaint and praise like Hannah and Sariah.

Mormon and Israel: Wealth

Walker Wright

Mormon's entire life was consumed by war and violence brought about by what he saw as divisions created by wealth, vanity, and economic inequality. His abridgment of the Nephite records often highlights the pride of the rich and inequality as the source of conflict. Yet, the patriarch Jacob—later renamed Israel[1]—is depicted in the Genesis account as being very prosperous and often pursuing wealth at the expense of others.

* * * * * * *

MORMON: Prior to the coming of the Messiah, my people were divided against themselves over their riches, bringing about vast inequality in the land.[2] Even the coming of the resurrected Lord could not keep the temptations of wealth at bay for long. My people became prosperous once more, leading to pride, class distinctions, avarice, and the rise of competing political affiliations.[3] Even the people of Nephi were seduced by the allure of wealth.[4] The arrogance and inequality brought about by riches was at the root of the violent downfall of my people. Given these destructive results, how is it that you could devote so much of your life to the pursuit of wealth?[5]

---

1. Genesis 35:10.
2. 3 Nephi 6:10–14.
3. 4 Nephi 1:23–27; 35–38.
4. 4 Nephi 1:43.
5. See Genesis 30:31–32:5.

ISRAEL: My riches were not my own, but gifts from God. Not only was I blessed with prosperity,[6] but my father Isaac[7] and his father Abraham[8] also were. You claim my house, my covenant, and the heritage of my son Joseph,[9] yet in your vilifying of riches and the wealthy, you implicitly disparage the very patriarchs of the nation of Israel. Do not your own records maintain that God will cause His people to prosper in the land if they are faithful to their covenants?[10]

MORMON: Yes, but what do these covenants entail? In laying the foundational charter of Nephite society, our forefather and king Nephi drew on the words of Isaiah to demonstrate that we must deal justly with the poor. Those who do not are under the Lord's judgment.[11] It is prosperity for all, not a handful of elites. Nephi's brother Jacob, who was ordained and consecrated by Nephi himself, cautioned, "But wo unto the rich. . . . For because they are rich they despise the poor, and they persecute the meek, and their hearts are upon their treasures; wherefore, their treasure is their god. And behold, their treasure shall perish with them also."[12]

ISRAEL: This same Jacob, who is my namesake, taught your people that they should seek the kingdom of God first and then pursue riches with the intent of caring for the needy and the vulnerable.[13] This is akin to the

---

6. Genesis 27:28; 30:43.

7. Genesis 26:2–3; 12–14.

8. Genesis 13:2; 15:1; 24:34–35.

9. 3 Nephi 5:20–26.

10. See 1 Nephi 2:20; 4:14.

11. See 2 Nephi 13:14–26; 15:7–9; 20:1–3. "Perhaps the most difficult part of the Book of Mormon to explain is the inclusion of twelve entire chapters of Isaiah. These seemingly diverse sections may be unified by Nephi's effort to provide a defining charter for the new community. . . . In particular, the Isaiah quotations that Nephi selected form the basis for his prophetic blessing (2 Ne. 25–33) and also reiterate the social and economic principles characterizing Yahweh's people. Isaiah emphasizes that those who seek wealth and ignore the poor are departing from Yahweh's ways (2 Ne. 15). Adopting Isaiah's commentary as a charter for a community puts egalitarianism as a foundational principle. Nephi establishes an ideal with which Nephite society struggles throughout the Book of Mormon." Brant A. Gardner, *Traditions of the Fathers: The Book of Mormon as History* (Salt Lake City: Greg Kofford Books, 2015), 188–89.

12. 2 Nephi 9:30.

13. Jacob 2:17–19.

original covenant with my grandfather Abraham (Abram at the time): not only would he be blessed, but it was imperative that he should be a blessing unto others.[14] This is the context of his wealth, and he lived this ideal in his everyday life. For example, he displayed great hospitality by bringing three foreign strangers into his home and presenting them with a lavish feast.[15] He would have been unable to provide for his divine company had he not possessed the resources. His own charity and that of his nephew Lot are contrasted with the inhospitality of the people of Sodom and Gomorrah.[16] It is not wealth itself, but how it is used. Surely you must see this.

MORMON: While wealth can be used responsibly, too often it leads to conflict and wickedness.[17] Think of your father Isaac's disputes with the Philistines over his wells, livestock, and harvested goods.[18]

ISRAEL: The disputations only occurred because the Philistines were envious of my father's capital. This malice drove them to vandalize his property by filling up his wells. They even ran him off the land because he had supposedly become "mightier" than them due to his substance and influence.[19] To blame my father's wealth for their covetous hearts is to excuse the choices of the Philistines and condemn the blessings of the Lord. Despite all this, however, my father and the Philistines eventually found themselves on good terms with both parties possessing two wells each.[20]

MORMON: Yet, your father's situation demonstrates that peace can only come by relinquishing one's wealth. Isaac did not fight over his riches but

---

14. Genesis 12:1–3. "God offers a threefold blessing for Abram: God will bless him, he will be a blessing, and he will be a channel of blessing. The first means that Abram will come under God's care, protection, and favor. This will bring him safety and prosperity. The second means that Abram will provide care and protection to those in favor with him. Lot is an example in chapter 14. The third means that God will bring blessing to other people through Abram and his family." John H. Walton, *The NIV Application Commentary: Genesis* (Grand Rapids, Mich.: Zondervan, 2001), 399.

15. Genesis 18:1–8.

16. See Genesis 18:20–19:29; Ezekiel 16:49–50.

17. See Alma 4:6–12.

18. Genesis 26:12–22.

19. Genesis 26:14–16.

20. Genesis 26:17–22; 32–33.

simply left the land as asked and even honored the Philistines' claims on the wells.[21]

ISRAEL: But it was only *after* the Philistines realized that my father's wealth was a blessing from the Lord that they approached him to make a covenant of peace.[22] Had they not come to this realization, it is likely that the Philistines would have continued in their thievery. Following the treaty, my father's servants found his second well,[23] providing further evidence that God looks after our material well-being.

MORMON: But your observation of the Philistines only strengthens my original point: wealth tends to result in "envyings and strife."[24] You of all people should know this: your father-in-law Laban exploited you for twenty years, breaking the terms of your work contract and changing your wages multiple times.[25] His lust for material wealth warped his relationship with you, making him more of a master than kin.[26] He knowingly swindled you when he gave you Leah instead of Rachel in exchange for your first seven years of labor. He then extracted another seven years from you in order to obtain Rachel as a wife.[27] All this so that he might turn a profit.

ISRAEL: It is true that Laban's greed led him to cheat me, but we must not overlook how God rectified this unjust situation: He saw fit to bless me with a large portion of Laban's cattle.[28] Recall that your king Nephi declared that "the Lord was with us" when his people did "prosper exceedingly."[29] The tendency of the God of my fathers to bless his followers with affluence betrays your notion that riches are to be avoided. If the Lord expected me to shun such an abundance of goods, He surely would not have blessed me with them.

---

21. Genesis 26:17; 20–22.
22. Genesis 26:28.
23. Genesis 26:31–33.
24. Alma 1:32; see also Helaman 13:22.
25. Genesis 31:5–7, 41.
26. Genesis 29:14–15.
27. Genesis 29:16–27.
28. Genesis 30:32–43; 31:4–13.
29. 2 Nephi 5:9–13.

MORMON: But you obtained Laban's cattle through subtle trickery. Divinely inspired or not, you had to engage in the same craftiness as Laban. You both sought to "get gain": the very desire that gave rise to one of the most murderous secret combinations in my people's history as well as the eventual undoing of our civilization.[30] Such desire corrupts integrity[31] and often leads to "robbing and plundering."[32]

ISRAEL: According to your son Moroni, this same desire to "get gain" drove the "exceedingly industrious" Jaredites under Lib to "work all manner of fine work" until it was said that "never could be a people more blessed than they, and more prospered by the hand of the Lord."[33] This same Lord blessed me for my own earnest drive and I was able to leave Laban's company along with my family. I simply did as your record's own Amulek encouraged us to do: pray unto God that our crops may prosper and our flocks may increase.[34]

MORMON: You may remember that the division between the Nephites and Lamanites began early on with the struggle between Nephi and his brothers Laman and Lemuel. The latter "murmured" because their father Lehi "had led them out of the land of Jerusalem, to leave the land of their inheritance, and their gold, and their silver, and their precious things."[35] They complained to Nephi for their "suffer[ing] in the wilderness, which time we might have enjoyed our possession and the land of our inheritance; yea, and we might have been happy."[36] Their hearts were set on their earthly treasures rather than on the Lord. This created an ever-increasing divide that ended in the formation of two warring nations. This is why the resurrected Lord instructed, "Lay not up for yourselves treasures upon earth. . . . But lay up for yourselves treasures in heaven. . . . For where your treasure is, there will your heart be also."[37]

---

30. See Helaman 2:12–14; 6:17–18.
31. See Alma 11:1–3, 20.
32. Alma 17:14.
33. Ether 10:22–28; compare 4 Nephi 1:16.
34. Alma 34:20–25.
35. 1 Nephi 2:11.
36. 1 Nephi 17:21.
37. 3 Nephi 13:19–21.

ISRAEL: How easily you overlook the fact that those treasures were the property of Lehi.[38] His obtainment of riches obviously did not cause him to share the gross materialism of his sons. If being rich was such a risk, the Lord surely would not have chosen Lehi as his spokesman. Yet, God called one of my descendants[39] who seemed to be modeled after me, my father, and grandfather in regard to his wealth and obedience. Do you mean to suggest that the Lord made a mistake when he chose the wealthy Lehi as his prophet?

MORMON: Of course not. Lehi demonstrated that his heart was set on the Lord rather than money when he left his riches behind in obedience to a revelatory dream.[40] Nonetheless, the pursuit and embrace of wealth can set off a dangerous cycle. Your own life is a prime example. First, you took advantage of your elder brother Esau while he was in a weakened condition and convinced him to sell his birthright to you.[41]

ISRAEL: Esau obviously did not value or understand the significance of his birthright.[42] If he did, he would not have been so willing to sell it. If anything, I was rescuing something sacred from one who would profane it. Do not judge me for profiting from his flippancy, especially since it benefited my posterity (including you).

MORMON: I mean no disrespect nor do I wish to revoke the blessings of your inheritance. I simply want to point out how this initial desire for gain set off a chain of events. You not only stripped him of his birthright, which entitled you to a double portion,[43] but you went even further by seeking to deceive your elderly father into pronouncing Esau's blessing on you in his place.[44]

ISRAEL: That was my mother's idea.[45]

---

38. 1 Nephi 2:4; 3:16.
39. 1 Nephi 5:14; Alma 10:3.
40. 1 Nephi 2:1–4.
41. Genesis 25:29–33.
42. Genesis 25:34.
43. See Deuteronomy 21:17.
44. Genesis 27:18–29.
45. Genesis 27:5–17. "Jacob masquerades as Esau and wins his blind father's deathbed blessing. It is Rebekah who is responsible for concocting this act of

MORMON: Fine. You *and* your mother conspired to deceive Isaac. By doing so you received what was intended for Esau: "the dew of heaven, and the fatness of the earth, and plenty of corn and wine" along with the service and reverence of the nations.[46] You betrayed your brother and father to the point that Esau sought to have you killed![47] Even the Lamanite's false belief that they had been "wronged" and "robbed" of their inheritance produced within them an "eternal hatred towards the children of Nephi" to the point of murder and plundering.[48] The conflicts over wealth and power tear people apart. It nearly destroyed your own family. And these woes and struggles followed you throughout your entire life.

ISRAEL: Are you forgetting my generous gift to Esau prior to our meeting and reconciliation?[49] The night before, I prayed for deliverance, acknowledging God's hand in my prosperity.[50] Then I sent ahead over 550 animals in order to appease Esau and sway him from his murderous intent. While we originally fought over these riches, through them we were eventually brought together.

MORMON: But Esau at first refused your gift.[51] The way he embraced you when he saw you after so many years indicates that he had forgiven you prior to your generosity.[52]

---

deception. . . . Jacob is reluctant to go along with the ruse. He objects: [Gen. 27:11–12]. But Rebekah insists, claiming that if there is a curse it will fall on her. . . . It is she who makes the savory food; it is she who takes Esau's garments and puts them on Jacob; it is she who thrusts the food into his hand. Once inside Isaac's room, Jacob is left to carry out his mother's act of deception on his own. . . . But how does the narrator judge what Jacob has done? Does he share Isaac's and Esau's condemnation of Jacob? It is by no means clear that he does. He has gone to great effort to make Rebekah the instigator of the whole affair. Jacob is drawn into the deceptive scheme, but only reluctantly." Carl D. Evans, "The Patriarch Jacob: An 'Innocent Man,'" in *Abraham & Family: New Insights into the Patriarchal Narratives*, ed. Hershel Shanks (Washington, D.C.: Biblical Archaeology Society, 2000), 125–27.

46. Genesis 27:28–29.
47. Genesis 27:41.
48. Mosiah 10:12–18.
49. Genesis 32:11–20.
50. Genesis 32:9–12.
51. Genesis 33:8–9.
52. Genesis 33:4.

ISRAEL: We both were certainly overwhelmed with emotion, but I was wary of his refusal. I made sure that Esau accepted my gift as *indicative* of our reconciliation. He further recognized my riches as the grace of God.[53] And it was God's grace in the form of abundant wealth that saved my family and consequently the nation of Israel.

MORMON: How so?

ISRAEL: My son Joseph was promoted to vizier in Egypt after his interpretations of Pharaoh's dreams.[54] He predicted an economic cycle of seven plentiful years and seven years of famine. He made preparations to store up the excess of Egypt's harvest.[55] His financial management made the country rich in a time of scarcity. It was because of this surplus that my other sons ventured to Egypt to acquire food.[56]

MORMON: But Joseph was in Egypt because your other sons sold him into slavery.[57] Your favoritism toward Joseph bred jealousy among your children.[58] This preference for Joseph was spawned by your love for Rachel, your favorite wife. And it was Laban's initial deceit that propagated contention, ill will, and unhealthy competition between your wives.[59] This rivalry would carry over and manifest itself in the next generation between Joseph and his brothers. Do you see now? The lust for riches can have ramifications that cross generations. This is why wealth is so dangerous.

---

53. Genesis 33:10–11.
54. Genesis 41:1–45.
55. Genesis 41:46–57.
56. Genesis 42:1–7.
57. Genesis 37:18–36.
58. Genesis 37:2–4.
59. Genesis 29:30–30:24. "In Genesis 29, Laban is not only willing to cheat Jacob, but he also seems to lack any concern about the fate of his daughters. Leah ends up as 'unloved' or 'hated' (29:31). Rachel's marriage will be forever marred by the presence of her sister. A bitter rivalry will develop between the two, which will influence relationships into the next generation. All this, sacrificed for the sake of selfish gain. Laban's actions are clear testimony to the strong pull of material advancement in the detriment of human relationships." Paul D. Vrolijk, *Jacob's Wealth: An Examination into the Nature and Role of Material Possessions in the Jacob-Cycle (Gen 25:19 – 35:29)* (Leiden/Boston: Brill, 2011), 150.

ISRAEL: It was only by accumulating this supposedly dangerous wealth that Joseph was able to save Egypt, Israel (including my family), and other foreign nations from starvation and poverty. The surplus allowed him to open up exchange with both Egyptians and foreigners.[60] This was at least a partial fulfillment of Abraham's blessing: "And in thy seed shall all the nations of the earth be blessed."[61] I was reunited with my son whom I believed was dead, our family was reconciled, and we were saved.[62] Though my sons intended harm and "thought evil against" Joseph, "God meant it unto good, to bring to pass . . . to save much people alive."[63] *This* is how God's grace saved my family and the nation of Israel.

MORMON: If only those with wealth and power sought to help those in need, as King Benjamin taught us to do.[64] Unfortunately, it is my experience that they do not. Wealth too often begets greed, treachery, and carnage. We begin to objectify others and see them simply as instruments by which to gratify our excess.[65] The wickedness of my people was born out of this material gluttony[66] until it reached a point to where I could not even "recommend them unto God lest he should smite me."[67] We must seek to avoid both riches and their temptations. As our Lord said, "Ye cannot serve God and Mammon."[68]

ISRAEL: Mormon, this has nothing to do with serving mammon and everything to do with God's covenantal promises.[69] Of course the pursuit

---

60. Genesis 41:54–57; 47:13–26.

61. Genesis 22:18; compare Genesis 12:1–3.

62. Genesis 45–46.

63. Genesis 50:20.

64. See Mosiah 4:16–26.

65. Psychologist Tim Kasser has found "that materialistic values not only undermine the well-being of those who strongly hold them, but also negatively affect the health and happiness of many others. When interactions with people are based on such values, less empathy and intimacy are present in relationships, and materialistic values are more likely to be transmitted to the next generation. The broader community will also be damaged when those in power objectify others in their pursuit of wealth and status." Tim Kasser, *The High Price of Materialism* (Cambridge, Mass.: MIT Press, 2002), 95.

66. See 4 Nephi 1:23–26.

67. Moroni 9:21.

68. 3 Nephi 13:24.

69. See Deuteronomy 28:1–13.

of wealth can be disastrous. I experienced it firsthand, as you pointed out. But inherent in the *shalom* of God is peace and prosperity.[70] No longer is one plagued by desperation and consumed by the anxieties of poverty. Instead, abundance allows one to focus on God and our fellow man in security, peace, and gratitude.[71] The Lord intends for us to flourish. We should seek after these blessings and then graciously accept them by being faithful stewards.

---

70. See Psalms 35:27 and 147:14. "The Hebrew word for peace . . . is derived from a root denoting wholeness or completeness, and its frame of reference throughout Jewish literature is bound up with the notion of . . . perfection. Its significance is thus not limited to the political domain-to the absence of war and enmity-or to the social-to the absence of quarrel and strife. It ranges over several spheres and can refer in different contexts to bounteous physical conditions, to a moral value, and, ultimately, to a cosmic principle and divine attribute. In the Bible, the word *shalom* is most commonly used to refer to a *state of affairs*, one of well-being, tranquility, prosperity, and security, circumstances unblemished by any sort of defect. *Shalom* is a blessing, a manifestation of divine grace." Aviezar Ravitzky, "Peace," *20th Century Jewish Religious Thought: Original Essays on Critical Concepts, Movements, and Beliefs*, ed. Arthur Cohen, Paul Mendes-Flohr (Philadelphia: Jewish Publication Society, 2009), 685.

71. Recent research suggests that affluence actually led to the rise of ascetic and moralizing religions during the Axial Age. Several reasons for this connection have been proposed. First, greater prosperity provided both the time and resources to develop more abstract forms of religion. It also brought about increased urbanization and consequently more cosmopolitan, diverse societies. Finally, the increase in societal wealth "may have triggered a drastic change in strategies, shifting motivations away from materialistic goals (acquiring more wealth, higher social status) and short-term aggressive strategies ('an eye for an eye'), typical of fast life strategies, toward long-term investment in reciprocation ('do unto others') and in self-development (variously described as the 'good life' or 'self-actualization' in Maslow's original theory)." Nicolas Baumer, Alexandre Hyafill, Ian Morris, and Pascal Boyer, "Increased Affluence Explains the Emergence of Ascetic Wisdoms and Moralizing Religions," *Current Biology* 25, no. 1 (2015): 12–13.

Master and Disciple: Communication

Benjamin Peters and *John Durham Peters*

DISCIPLE: Master, I am troubled. Teach me. How are we to communicate? The world is beset by a jumble of noisy voices clamoring in the wilderness. We see people rushing to and fro—we are like a ship of immigrants, lost at sea, seeking to out-shout our fellows and to spill over the sides to be the first to dry ground, where there is in fact none! How deafening the roar of the ocean and human noise competing, and worse still the silence of the world in response.

MASTER: What has been taught?

DISCIPLE (*pointing in the direction of Tiberias*): On the mount, it was spoken: "But let your communication be, Yea, yea; Nay, nay: for whatsoever is more than these cometh of evil."

MASTER: What does this saying mean?

DISCIPLE: I do not know. Some say that it means that words should be as simple as possible. That every statement should court the asymptote of clear statement, that every signal we send should be true, that redundancy is blessed—no more and no less.

MASTER: What do others say about this teaching?

DISCIPLE: They insist that our saying applies only to the integrity of our vows—that our "yes" should mean yes, and our "no" should mean no. They say that communication is good only when our speech expresses our commitment to act in a certain way, and we then act accordingly. Happy communication consists in purity of heart.

MASTER: What, then, do you, my friend, make of my saying that our communication should be yea, yea; nay, nay?

DISCIPLE: Of course our interactions should be straightforward and honest as possible, but saying this is not enough. I cannot believe that all communication must be simple, for I cannot see it in your teaching. You have spoken of a sower, who joyously spreads seeds without regard to where they land. The sower suggests that words are not fully formed and ready for exchange in the economy of mutually forming minds so much as seeds cast onto various soils. The destiny of the seed depends on luck and chance and the cultivation of the willing listener. You have declared, "those who have ears to hear, let them hear!" The sower suggests that the harvest of words is to those with ears to reap, not to voices to plant. And your parables, which you toss aside to friend and foe as freely as your sower does, are infinitely interpretable to those that receive them. If this is so, it cannot be that communication should be only yea, yea; nay, nay.

MASTER: What else do you make of this interpretation?

DISCIPLE: I have no quarrel with purity of heart, but it seems very much a private thing, not a matter that can be shared at all, and hence not a likely basis for communication. A pure heart cannot be proclaimed, and even less can it be shown. Woe unto those who make a show of their own goodness. The pure heart never knows it is pure; only a penitent heart full of the feeling of its own weakness is ever pure. And it is only in rare moments that we make promises, oaths, and commitments; many of our greatest promises we make only once in a lifetime, and yet every day we speak hundreds and thousands of words full of much more information than just yes or no. How can the exception set the norm? Here we are no closer to understanding how to communicate. Of course we should keep our word; of course our acts make true our words. The interpretation is so self-evident it is of little help.

  There is also the trouble of putting that self-evident truth—that honesty is good—into practice. You can hardly even say it, let alone live it. The most honest person can never say I am honest without running the risk of thereby becoming a liar. It takes no great mind—in fact it may take a particularly small kind of mind—to realize that every interaction with others demands negotiation and compromise, and in fact benefits from the graceful silences, polite evasions, and ethical redirections that oil social life. Examples abound: Would it be evil to respond to a stranger's greeting cheerfully, when in fact our day is glum? Would a loving husband always say the first thing he is thinking when his wife asks his thoughts? What is kind and what is true are not always the same. You yourself have encouraged us to dissimulate, to look chipper and presentable when we are fasting so that no one will know. No, Master, I cannot fully accept this interpretation. How blessed are those that do not speak in binary true or false statements, and how cursed are those who can speak only along the strait and narrow! The lots and dice may speak this way, but not people or God.

No, Master, you must mean something else. You see from my questions how even the plainest way of stating that we should speak plainly is anything but self-evident and calls forth more inquiry. Perhaps you mean that good communication and the grander coupling of human lives should best be carried out in two-way dialogue—that one mind might be able to contend, yea, and that another, nay? Perhaps, you mean to instruct us in the goodness of the social relations that bind together human beings—to recognize the greater embrace that circumscribes all truth forged in the back and forth of two fellows in *chavruta* one with another? Perhaps in yea, yea, nay, nay, we find the key that in hashing out the details and differences in our views, we are in fact engaging in an activity of forming and expressing truth worthy of your divine approval? Does not God invite us to wrestle with him and to haggle over truth with each other?

MASTER: Would you then see this conversation too as circumscribing some greater truth we could not see before?

DISCIPLE: Master, I take it that you would teach me this: that without you, there would be no dialogue, and without dialogue, there would be no further interpretation of your teaching.

MASTER:

DISCIPLE: Have I understood your will? Has my interpretation fulfilled your teaching?

MASTER:

DISCIPLE: (*Pauses.*) Am I to understand that by your silence, you are showing me our conversation is at an end, and that by force of ending the conversation, and leaving me without reconciliation, I am in fact justified in believing that dialogue between two minds is the higher understanding of your teaching that good communication is no more than yea, yea; nay, nay?

(*Pauses.*) Perhaps even your kingdom is built on a series of asymmetrical pairs—child-parent, spouse-spouse, disciple-teacher—so that we might learn to develop a more divine disposition in dialogue with the other?

The master turns and walks away . . .

DISCIPLE: Master, where are you going?

Master, how can I know the truth of your teaching if you will not confirm it?

Master, where is the simplicity of your teaching if you will not utter even a yea, yea or nay, nay in reply?

Master, where is the honesty of your commitment to me as my master, if you will abandon me in my time of need?

Master, I now assume I was wrong, although I do not know why. It cannot be that divine communication is paved with dialogue, if you would abandon me without resolution in the middle of it. Either you have done so because you are indeed no master or because dialogue is not itself divine; with or without you, I cannot know for sure.

(*Disciple turns to himself.*) Master . . . where are you?

(*Master's voice echoes inside disciple's mind.*) Where are you? Are you sure you know where you are? How could it be that dialogue is divine? Have I not taught in the same parables that it is up to each person to hear alone? Have I not responded to almost every question with another question?

(*Internal dialogue continues in Master's voice.*) The higher law is neither an eye for an eye, nor a word for a word. Nay, nay: you have misunderstood my teaching. I have never left you for I have never been with you—at least not as you think I have. Dialogue is no higher form of communication. Every conversation consists of two partners who are already in conversation with themselves. Every dialogue is left part way through. We are not one—nor should we wish to be. The clamor that besets us at every turn cannot be healed by communication; in our search for better communication, we get the question all wrong. The question is not how can we better communicate with others, but how our lives together may mean something more. The clamor that is hardest to still is not that which enters the eyes and ears from the noisy bazaar of human affairs but from the ceaseless words that work their way out from every mouth. Even God speaks in whispers and in silence. We have yet to confront so central and salutary feature of the human lot as the fact that our dialogues never resolve or connect in words, but in love. This is our end blessing. We can never teach, except when we begin again to see others not as ourselves, but as themselves, separate, solitary, worthy of love in their full particularities. And when we see that, we too are only others amid all the others. To see the self as an other and the other as a self: this is the heart of my, or rather our, teaching.

The Authors

Michael Austin is Executive Vice President for Academic Affairs at the University of Evansville in Evansville, Indiana. He is the author or editor of ten books, including *Peculiar Portrayals: Mormons on the Page, Stage, and Screen* (Utah State University Press, 2010). His book, *Re-reading Job: Understanding the Ancient World's Greatest Poem* (Greg Kofford Books, 2014), was awarded the 2014 Association for Mormon Letters Award for religious non-fiction. He lives in southern Indiana with his wife, Karen, and their children, Porter and Clarissa.

Mark T. Decker has a Ph.D. in American Literature from The Pennsylvania State University. He is Associate Professor and Assistant Department Chair in Bloomsburg University's Department of English. He is co-editor of *Peculiar Portrayals: Mormons on the Page, Stage, and Screen* (Utah State University Press, 2010) and the author of *Industrial Society and the Science Fiction Blockbuster: Social Critique in Films of Lucas, Scott and Cameron* (McFarland, 2016).

Nicholas J. Frederick received a Ph.D. in the History of Christianity from Claremont Graduate University in 2013. He currently holds a position as Assistant Professor of Ancient Scripture in the Department of Religion at Brigham Young University. He and his wife Julie reside in Spanish Fork, Utah, with their four children, Miranda, Samuel, Kassandra, and Madelyn.

Heather Hardy earned an M.B.A. from Brigham Young University and worked for several years in university administration at Yale and BYU before leaving the workforce to raise a family and pursue a life of learning. Heather currently serves as Primary president in her Asheville, North Carolina ward. She and her husband Grant are the parents of two children.

Ronan James Head lives in Malvern, Worcestershire, England, and has degrees from the University of Birmingham, the University of Oxford, and The Johns Hopkins University. From the latter he earned a Ph.D. in

Near Eastern Studies in 2011. He currently teaches theology and philosophy at a private cathedral school in England.

James D. Holt is Senior Lecturer in Religious Education at the University of Chester, U.K. He holds a Ph.D. in Mormon Theology from the University of Liverpool. He lives in Manchester, England, and is married with four children. He is the author of *Religious Education in the Secondary School: An Introduction to Teaching, Learning and the World Religions* (Routledge, 2015).

Jason A. Kerr is Assistant Professor of English at Brigham Young University, where he teaches the Bible as Literature and courses in Early Modern British Literature. He has published articles on Milton's scriptural theology and is currently working on a book about Richard Baxter's political theology of consent. He lives in Provo with his wife Kristine and their children, Julia and Elijah.

Jared Ludlow is an Associate Professor in the Ancient Scripture department at Brigham Young University where he has been teaching since 2006. Prior to that, he taught Religion and History at BYU-Hawaii for six years. He received his Ph.D. from the University of California–Berkeley and the Graduate Theological Union in Near Eastern Religions focusing on Second Temple Judaism.

Steven L. Peck is Associate Professor in the Biology Department of Brigham Young University and has published over 50 scientific articles in the area of evolutionary ecology. He has also published award-winning fiction and poetry in a variety of places. His novel, *The Scholar of Moab* (Torrey House, 2011), was the Association of Mormon Letters best novel of 2011. A collection of his short stories, *Wandering Realities*, was recently published by Zarahemla Books (2015), and a collection of his essays on science and religion, called *Evolving Faith*, is part of the Neal A. Maxwell's Living Faith Series (2015). He lives in Pleasant Grove, Utah, with his wife, Lori Peck. They have five children.

Julie M. Smith graduated from the University of Texas at Austin with a B.A. in English and from the Graduate Theological Union in Berkeley, California, with an M.A. in Biblical Studies. She is on the executive board of the Mormon Theology Seminar and the steering committee for the

BYU New Testament Commentary, for which she is writing a commentary on the Gospel of Mark. She is the author of *Search, Ponder, and Pray: A Guide to the Gospels* (Greg Kofford Books, 2014). She lives near Austin, Texas, where she homeschools her three children. She also blogs for Times and Seasons, where she is the book review editor.

Joseph M. Spencer is Visiting Assistant Professor of Ancient Scripture at Brigham Young University. He's the author of *An Other Testament* (Maxwell Institute Press, 2016) and *For Zion: A Mormon Theology of Hope* (Greg Kofford Books, 2014), as well as the forthcoming, *The Vision of All: Twenty-Five Lectures on Isaiah in Nephi's Record* (Greg Kofford Books, 2016). He currently serves as the associate director of the Mormon Theology Seminar and as an associate editor of the *Journal of Book of Mormon Studies*. He and Karen, his wife, live with their five children in Provo, Utah.

Walter E. A. van Beek is a Dutch cultural anthropologist with a large field experience in West Africa. He performed fieldwork among the Kapsiki/Higi of North Cameroon and Northeastern Nigeria, and among the Dogon of Mali, for over four decades. On the religions of both groups he has published extensively. He held the chair of Anthropology of Religion at Tilburg University and is Senior Researcher at the African Studies Centre, Leiden University. In biblical studies his main interest is the Old Testament, for which his African experience is a major inspiration. As a Latter-day Saint he has served in many ecclesiastical positions, such as branch president and stake president.

Miranda Wilcox is Associate Professor of English at Brigham Young University in Provo, Utah, where she teaches medieval literature. Her research focuses on the intersections of religious and textual culture in early medieval Europe, especially in Anglo-Saxon England. She is co-editor with John D. Young of *Standing Apart: Mormon Historical Consciousness and the Concept of Apostasy* (Oxford University Press, 2014). She received a master's and doctorate in medieval studies from the University of Notre Dame.

Walker A. Wright graduated from the University of North Texas with an M.B.A. in Strategic Management and a B.B.A. in Organizational Behavior and Human Resource Management. He has been published in *SquareTwo* and *BYU Studies Quarterly*. His online writing can be found at the blogs

Difficult Run, Worlds Without End, and Times and Seasons. He lives in Denton, Texas, with his wife.

Benjamin Peters is a media scholar, the author of *How Not to Network a Nation: The Uneasy History of the Soviet Internet* (MIT Press, 2016), and the editor of *Digital Keywords: A Vocabulary of Information Society and Culture* (Princeton, 2016). He is Assistant Professor of Communication at the University of Tulsa and affiliated faculty at the Information Society Project at Yale Law School. A wannabe frisbeeist, he is also a husband and father of four. He can be found online at petersbenjamin.wordpress.com and on twitter at @bjpeters.

John Durham Peters teaches at the University of Iowa and is the author most recently of *The Marvelous Clouds: Toward a Philosophy of Elemental Media* (University of Chicago, 2015). He is also a wannabee frisbeeist, husband, father of two, and grandfather of four.

Also available from
GREG KOFFORD BOOKS

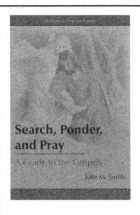

Search, Ponder, and Pray:
A Guide to the Gospels

Julie M. Smith

Paperback, ISBN: 978-1-58958-671-0
Hardcover, ISBN: 978-1-58958-672-7

From the author's preface:

During my graduate studies in theology, I came to realize that there is quite a bit of work done in the field of biblical studies that can be useful to members of the Church as they read the scriptures. Unfortunately, academic jargon usually makes these works impenetrable, and I was unable to find many publications that made this research accessible to the non-specialist. In this book, I have endeavored to present some of the most interesting insights of biblical scholars—in plain language.

It was also important to me that I not present the work of these scholars in a way that would make you feel obligated to accept their conclusions. Since scholars rarely agree with each other, I can see no reason why you should feel compelled to agree with them. My hope is that the format of this book will encourage you to view the insights of scholars as the beginning of a discussion instead of the end of an argument. In some cases, I have presented the positions of scholars (and even some critics of the Church) specifically to encourage you to develop your own responses to these arguments based on your personal scripture study. I certainly don't agree with every idea in this book.

I encourage you to read the Introduction. Although I have endeavored to keep it as short as possible, there are several issues related to the interpretation of the scriptures that should be addressed before you begin interpreting.

It is my experience that thoughtful scripture study leads to personal revelation. I hope that through the process of searching the scriptures, pondering these questions, and praying about the answers, you will be edified.

Life is full of unanswered questions. Here are over 4,500 more of them.

Re-reading Job: Understanding the Ancient World's Greatest Poem

Michael Austin

Paperback, ISBN: 978-1-58958-667-3
Hardcover, ISBN: 978-1-58958-668-0

Job is perhaps the most difficult to understand of all books in the Bible. While a cursory reading of the text seems to relay a simple story of a righteous man whose love for God was tested through life's most difficult of challenges and rewarded for his faith through those trials, a closer reading of Job presents something far more complex and challenging. The majority of the text is a work of poetry that authors and artists through the centuries have recognized as being one of--if not the--greatest poem of the ancient world.

In *Re-reading Job: Understanding the Ancient World's Greatest Poem*, author Michael Austin shows how most readers have largely misunderstood this important work of scripture and provides insights that enable us to re-read Job in a drastically new way. In doing so, he shows that the story of Job is far more than that simple story of faith, trials, and blessings that we have all come to know, but is instead a subversive and complex work of scripture meant to inspire readers to rethink all that they thought they knew about God.

Praise for *Re-reading Job*:

"In this remarkable book, Michael Austin employs his considerable skills as a commentator to shed light on the most challenging text in the entire Hebrew Bible. Without question, readers will gain a deeper appreciation for this extraordinary ancient work through Austin's learned analysis. Rereading Job signifies that Latter-day Saints are entering a new age of mature biblical scholarship. It is an exciting time, and a thrilling work." — David Bokovoy, author, *Authoring the Old Testament*

Authoring the Old Testament: Genesis–Deuteronomy

David Bokovoy

Paperback, ISBN: 978-1-58958-588-1
Hardcover, ISBN: 978-1-58958-675-8

For the last two centuries, biblical scholars have made discoveries and insights about the Old Testament that have greatly changed the way in which the authorship of these ancient scriptures has been understood. In the first of three volumes spanning the entire Hebrew Bible, David Bokovoy dives into the Pentateuch, showing how and why textual criticism has led biblical scholars today to understand the first five books of the Bible as an amalgamation of multiple texts into a single, though often complicated narrative; and he discusses what implications those have for Latter-day Saint understandings of the Bible and modern scripture.

Praise for *Authoring the Old Testament*:

"*Authoring the Old Testament* is a welcome introduction, from a faithful Latter-day Saint perspective, to the academic world of Higher Criticism of the Hebrew Bible. . . . [R]eaders will be positively served and firmly impressed by the many strengths of this book, coupled with Bokovoy's genuine dedication to learning by study and also by faith." — John W. Welch, editor, *BYU Studies Quarterly*

"Bokovoy provides a lucid, insightful lens through which disciple-students can study intelligently LDS scripture. This is first rate scholarship made accessible to a broad audience—nourishing to the heart and mind alike." — Fiona Givens, co-author, *The God Who Weeps: How Mormonism Makes Sense of Life*

"I repeat: this is one of the most important books on Mormon scripture to be published recently. . . . [*Authoring the Old Testament*] has the potential to radically expand understanding and appreciation for not only the Old Testament, but scripture in general. It's really that good. Read it. Share it with your friends. Discuss it." — David Tayman, The Improvement Era: A Mormon Blog

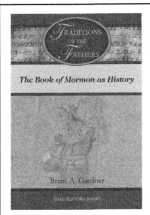

Traditions of the Fathers:
The Book of Mormon
as History

Brant A. Gardner

ISBN: 978-1-58958-665-9

2015 Best Religious Non-fiction Award
by the Association for Mormon Letters

"In the study of historical texts, context is king. Traditions of the Fathers masterfully contextualizes the diverse peoples of the Book of Mormon as they move, merge, and multiply across the Mesoamerican landscape. More than a simple lens, Gardner's multidisciplinary approach provides readers with illuminating, prismatic views of the Book of Mormon." — Mark Alan Wright, Assistant Professor of Ancient Scripture at Brigham Young University and Associate Editor of the *Journal of Book of Mormon Studies*

"The work he has done is rich, thorough, provocative. Like all Kofford books, this one is attractively produced, easy to hold in the hands and easy on the eyes. But best of all, it's informative, cogent, and altogether worth reading. I recommend it." — Julie J. Nichols, Association for Mormon Letters

Joseph Smith's Polygamy: Toward a Better Understanding

Brian C. Hales
and Laura H. Hales

Paperback, ISBN: 978-1-58958-723-6

In the last several years a wealth of information has been published on Joseph Smith's practice of polygamy. For some who were already well aware of this aspect of early Mormon history, the availability of new research and discovered documents has been a wellspring of further insight and knowledge into this topic. For others who are learning of Joseph's marriages to other women for the first time, these books and online publications (including the LDS Church's recent Gospel Topics essays on the subject) can be both an information overload and a challenge to one's faith.

In this short volume, Brian C. Hales (author of the 3-volume Joseph Smith's Polygamy set) and Laura H. Hales wade through the murky waters of history to help bring some clarity to this episode of Mormonism's past, examining both the theological explanations of the practice and the accounts of those who experienced it first hand. As this episode of Mormon history involved more than just Joseph and his first wife Emma, this volume also includes short biographies of the 36 women who were married to the Prophet but whose stories of faith, struggle, and courage have been largely forgotten and ignored over time. While we may never fully understand the details and reasons surrounding this practice, Brian and Laura Hales provide readers with an accessible, forthright, and faithful look into this challenging topic so that we can at least come toward a better understanding.

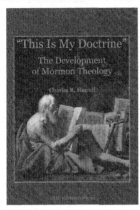

"This is My Doctrine":
The Development of Mormon
Theology

Charles R. Harrell

Hardcover, ISBN: 978-1-58958-103-6

The principal doctrines defining Mormonism today often bear little resemblance to those it started out with in the early 1830s. This book shows that these doctrines did not originate in a vacuum but were rather prompted and informed by the religious culture from which Mormonism arose. Early Mormons, like their early Christian and even earlier Israelite predecessors, brought with them their own varied culturally conditioned theological presuppositions (a process of convergence) and only later acquired a more distinctive theological outlook (a process of differentiation).

In this first-of-its-kind comprehensive treatment of the development of Mormon theology, Charles Harrell traces the history of Latter-day Saint doctrines from the times of the Old Testament to the present. He describes how Mormonism has carried on the tradition of the biblical authors, early Christians, and later Protestants in reinterpreting scripture to accommodate new theological ideas while attempting to uphold the integrity and authority of the scriptures. In the process, he probes three questions: How did Mormon doctrines develop? What are the scriptural underpinnings of these doctrines? And what do critical scholars make of these same scriptures? In this enlightening study, Harrell systematically peels back the doctrinal accretions of time to provide a fresh new look at Mormon theology.

"*This Is My Doctrine*" will provide those already versed in Mormonism's theological tradition with a new and richer perspective of Mormon theology. Those unacquainted with Mormonism will gain an appreciation for how Mormon theology fits into the larger Jewish and Christian theological traditions.

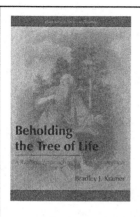

Beholding the Tree of Life:
A Rabbinic Approach to
the Book of Mormon

Bradley J. Kramer

Paperback, ISBN: 978-1-58958-701-4
Hardcover, ISBN: 978-1-58958-702-1

Too often readers approach the Book of Mormon simply as a collection of quotations, an inspired anthology to be scanned quickly and routinely recited. In Beholding the Tree of Life Bradley J. Kramer encourages his readers to slow down, to step back, and to contemplate the literary qualities of the Book of Mormon using interpretive techniques developed by Talmudic and post-Talmudic rabbis. Specifically, Kramer shows how to read the Book of Mormon closely, in levels, paying attention to the details of its expression as well as to its overall connection to the Hebrew Scriptures—all in order to better appreciate the beauty of the Book of Mormon and its limitless capacity to convey divine meaning.

Praise for *Authoring the Old Testament*:

"Latter-day Saints have claimed the Book of Mormon as the keystone of their religion, but it presents itself first and foremost as a Jewish narrative. *Beholding the Tree of Life* is the first book I have seen that attempts to situate the Book of Mormon by paying serious attention to its Jewish literary precedents and ways of reading scripture. It breaks fresh ground in numerous ways that enrich an LDS understanding of the scriptures and that builds bridges to a potential Jewish readership." — Terryl L. Givens, author of *By the Hand of Mormon: The American Scripture that Launched a New World Religion*

"Bradley Kramer has done what someone ought to have done long ago, used the methods of Jewish scripture interpretation to look closely at the Book of Mormon. Kramer has taken the time and put in the effort required to learn those methods from Jewish teachers. He explains what he has learned clearly and carefully. And then he shows us the fruit of that learning by applying it to the Book of Mormon. The results are not only interesting, they are inspiring. This is one of those books that, on reading it, I thought 'I wish I'd written that!'" — James E. Faulconer, author of *The Book of Mormon Made Harder* and *Faith, Philosophy, Scripture*

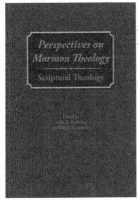

Perspectives on Mormon Theology: Scriptural Theology

Edited by James E. Faulconer and Joseph M. Spencer

Paperback, ISBN: 978-1-58958-712-0
Hardcover, ISBN: 978-1-58958-713-7

The phrase "theology of scripture" can be understood in two distinct ways. First, theology of scripture would be reflection on the nature of scripture, asking questions about what it means for a person or a people to be oriented by a written text (rather than or in addition to an oral tradition or a ritual tradition). In this first sense, theology of scripture would form a relatively minor part of the broader theological project, since the nature of scripture is just one of many things on which theologians reflect. Second, theology of scripture would be theological reflection guided by scripture, asking questions of scriptural texts and allowing those texts to shape the direction the theologian's thoughts pursue. In this second sense, theology of scripture would be less a part of the larger theological project than a way of doing theology, since whatever the theologian takes up reflectively, she investigates through the lens of scripture.

The essays making up this collection reflect attentiveness to both ways of understanding the phrase "theology of scripture." Each essay takes up the relatively un-self-conscious work of reading a scriptural text but then—at some point or another—asks the self-conscious question of exactly what she or he is doing in the work of reading scripture. We have thus attempted in this book (1) to create a dialogue concerning what scripture is for Latter-day Saints, and (2) to focus that dialogue on concrete examples of Latter-day Saints reading actual scripture texts.

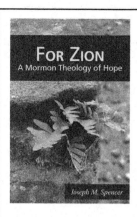

FOR ZION
A Mormon Theology of Hope

Joseph M. Spencer

For Zion:
A Mormon Theology of Hope

Joseph M. Spencer

Paperback, ISBN: 978-1-58958-568-3

What is hope? What is Zion? And what does it mean to hope for Zion? In this insightful book, Joseph Spencer explores these questions through the scriptures of two continents separated by nearly two millennia. In the first half, Spencer engages in a rich study of Paul's letter to the Roman to better understand how the apostle understood hope and what it means to have it. In the second half of the book, Spencer jumps to the early years of the Restoration and the various revelations on consecration to understand how Latter-day Saints are expected to strive for Zion. Between these halves is an interlude examining the hoped-for Zion that both thrived in the Book of Mormon and was hoped to be established again.

Praise for *For Zion*:

"Joseph Spencer is one of the most astute readers of sacred texts working in Mormon Studies. Blending theological savvy, historical grounding, and sensitive readings of scripture, he has produced an original and compelling case for consecration and the life of discipleship." — Terryl Givens, author, *Wrestling the Angel: The Foundations of Mormon Thought*

"*For Zion: A Mormon Theology of Hope* is more than a theological reflection. It also consists of able textual exegesis, historical contextualization, and philosophic exploration. Spencer's careful readings of Paul's focus on hope in Romans and on Joseph Smith's development of consecration in his early revelations, linking them as he does with the Book of Mormon, have provided an intriguing, intertextual avenue for understanding what true stewardship should be for us—now and in the future. As such he has set a new benchmark for solid, innovative Latter-day Saint scholarship that is at once provocative and challenging." — Eric D. Huntsman, author, *The Miracles of Jesus*

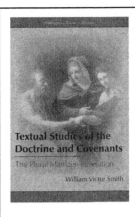

Textual Studies of
the Doctrine and Covenants:
The Plural Marriage Revelation

William Victor Smith

Paperback, ISBN: 978-1-58958-690-1
Hardcover, ISBN: 978-1-58958-691-8

The July 12, 1843 revelation was the last of Joseph Smith's formal written revelations, and it was a watershed in Mormonism for many reasons. *Textual Studies of the Doctrine and Covenants: The Plural Marriage Revelation* constitutes a study of the text of that revelation, its genetic profile as an endpoint for a number of trajectories in Mormon thought, liturgy, and priestly cosmology, and a brief exploration of its historical impact and interpretation.

CPSIA information can be obtained
at www.ICGtesting.com
Printed in the USA
FSOW03n0129290717
36717FS